Towers In The Light

Rebuilding The Liberal Christian Vision And The Mainline Church

James Albert Flurer

Fairway Press
Lima, Ohio

TOWERS IN THE LIGHT

FIRST EDITION

Library of Congress Catalog Card Number: 94-70688

ISBN 1-55673-931-1

PRINTED IN U.S.A.

To Brian,
Donald and Barclay

TABLE OF CONTENTS

FOREWORD

Underlying this beautifully written book is the conviction that a vital church must have an inspiring theological vision to undergird its ministries of caring for souls and seeking social justice. In developing this thesis, my friend and former student Jim Flurer has produced an excellent primer that can be read with pleasure and profit by many Christians. He believes that the liberal church has much to offer in these perilous and tumultuous times. He is also convinced that the liberal church is in trouble, partly because its message is unclear. All this matters to him greatly. In response he offers a constructive remedy. Jim writes with passion, clarity, and discernment. There is theological substance in these pages for he knows the subject well. Equally important is his skill in presenting difficult topics in a lucid and engaging fashion. No dry-as-dust, dull prose here. I envy his ability to make use of striking metaphors and to connect theological thinking with other human endeavors in a fascinating and illuminating way.

Of all the divisions among Protestant Christians, the most important may be the split between the "orthodox" and the "liberals." As imprecise as these terms are, they refer to two quite different ways of understanding the nature of religious truth. Orthodoxy assumes that truth has been given in the past once and for all in some more or less permanent form. Our task is to discover these "fundamentals" and to believe them without question. Liberals believe that religious truth has to be reconstructed for every new generation.

Earlier in this century, Harry Emerson Fosdick said that he wanted to be "a serious Christian and an intelligent modern." One could hardly express the aim of liberal Christians any better. Fosdick described the liberals of his generation as standing between the fundamentalists on the right and the humanists on the left. The fundamentalists, he said, thought that if you changed astronomies, the stars would be lost. The humanists had concluded that there were no stars and never had been. Liberals believed that the stars were still there, just as they always were, but astronomies must change as knowledge advances. Two fundamental assumptions underlie this distinction between abiding stars and changing astronomies. (1) All belief systems are human constructions that are historically relative and culturally conditioned. (2) A wide gap exists between the world view of the Bible and that of the modern world. This poses a difficult problem. How can a Bible written long ago and containing many outdated ideas provide a permanently valid revelation of God? The task of liberalism is to answer this question.

Jim Flurer's work is a worthy addition to the continuing task of revising astronomies without losing sight of the stars. I recommend his book enthusiastically.

Kenneth Cauthen
John Price Crozer Griffith Professor of Theology, emeritus
Colgate-Rochester/Bexley Hall/Crozer
Rochester, New York
February 25, 1994

INTRODUCTION

I write because I am deeply troubled about the state of Liberal Christianity. It is no secret the liberal church today suffers from disorder, demoralization and decline. Over the past 50 years, we have moved from the mainline to the sideline while conservatives like the Southern Baptists, Assemblies of God and The 700 Club seem to sweep all before them. More and more, when Americans think of "Christian" they think of Jerry Falwell, Jimmy Swaggart and Pat Robertson.

It seems the liberal Christian tradition is finished as a vital force in American life. Yet I believe today's troubles do not spell the end for the liberal, Mainline church. The current slide into obscurity can be reversed. And it must.

Yet how can this be done? In recent years, liberals have followed three broad strategies. First, the most important leaders in liberal thinking take experience as their starting point. Black, Feminist, Gay and Liberation theologies argue that if others would only accept the truth of their experience, all would be well. The result has been liberal theology's steady fragmentation and increasing confusion and anger among many people in the pews.

A second liberal approach has concentrated on process. This viewpoint believes that decline can be reversed with better techniques. If only we could learn how to train leaders more skillfully, persuasively recruit new members and effectively organize, all would be well. The result has been endless reorganization and training with little, if any, result.

The third and most popular approach is to ignore liberal decline. This viewpoint believes nothing need change within the church. If only more people would appreciate the church's virtues and come flocking in the doors, all would be well.

I suggest another option. Basic to everything that follows is the conviction that liberal Christians must reclaim our most fundamental beliefs and values. While continuing to applaud diversity, we must rebuild our overarching vision and make it the driving force behind Mainline church renewal.

Liberation theologies are important pieces of the liberal puzzle but they are not the whole puzzle. Effective techniques, training and organization are important but not as important as a powerful vision and knowing what needs to be done. As local churches struggle and finally close their doors, even the most stubborn traditionalists must admit that more of the same will not do.

Today, liberal, Mainline churches drift like an oceanliner cut from its moorings with no clear sense of purpose and direction. We are failing to pass on our tradition with clarity and passion. My own background is a case in point.

I grew up during the 1950's in suburban Philadelphia. My father's family were austere, logical Germans — Prussian rigor mixed with southern German simplicity. My maternal family was from the Caribbean island of Barbados. My father was Lutheran. My mother, Church of England. In America, we compromised and became Methodists.

As a child, I attended a neighborhood Methodist church. My introduction to Christianity there was both compelling and frustrating: enough to make me want more, not enough to satisfy emotionally or intellectually.

In 1966, I went off to Ursinus College, a small liberal arts school in Pennsylvania with a withering connection to the German Reformed tradition. At college, a few of my classmates guessed I was a serious seeker; most assumed I was an atheist. My skepticism was obvious; my piety was not. Although a history major, my searching sent me into religion courses during my junior year. I studied with Al Creager, a liberal pastor and teacher, *par excellence*. Finally, I minored in religion.

Then came the summer of 1968. King was dead. The war in Vietnam dragged on. Robert F. Kennedy ran for President. Until June 4, 1968, my future plans included law school, a Mercedes and a house on Philadelphia's Mainline. But that night I stayed up until the election returns from the California primary came in. I watched Kennedy's victory speech, then heard the news that Bobby, like his brother John, had been shot.

The prophet Isaiah tells us the word of the Lord came to him in a vision the year King Uzziah died. Although I claim no vision nor unique revelation, Robert Kennedy's death was the transforming moment of my life. The morning after his assassination, I was headed for seminary. With Bob Kennedy dead, the rest of us would have to do "something," however uncertain that "something" might be. A life of private gain was no longer an option.

For me, the natural course was, not the law, but the church. In the 1960's, the liberal church was the moral authority for change in America, the champion of civil rights, human dignity and peace. I applied to Crozer Theological Seminary because Martin Luther King, Jr., had been a graduate. I wanted to study with those who taught King. Learn what he had learned. The following year, Crozer moved from Chester, Pennsylvania, to become part of an ecumenical center in Rochester, New York, where the social gospel's founder, Walter Rauschenbusch, had taught. I decided to go along.

After graduation I was ordained by the United Church of Christ's Philadelphia Association, having parted company with the United Methodists three years before. I became pastor of two small churches in Pennsylvania's coal country. It was there I began to learn something was going wrong. I came to envy the Pentecostal preacher in the next town who knew exactly what should be done at his church. It was as if he had arrived with a blueprint that told him what to do and how to do it.

If there were blueprints available for liberal churches, I did not have one and I knew no one who did. It seemed, instead, liberal churches lived off the surplus of past glories. In the 1970's, we hardly noticed that decline had begun.

Eventually, I went back to the Divinity Schools in Rochester for post graduate study. Finally in 1979, I became chaplain at Bethany Children's Home, a UCC related institution in eastern Pennsylvania for abused and neglected boys and girls.

Here was a community of black, white, Hispanic, Asian and Native American children who had suffered terribly. As society's most vulnerable, they bore the spiritual and physical scars of the modern world's failures. A few came from religious backgrounds that were positive and sustaining. Some came fearing religion because of the contempt and condemnation it had hurled at them in the past. Most came with little religious background of any kind.

These children were a microcosm of our modern world: pluralistic, multiracial, multicultural and, for the most part, secular. Yet almost all came with the burning spiritual questions and struggles of our time. If the world is the way they teach in science class, how can there be a God? If God is so smart, so good and so powerful, why is there so much evil and suffering? Are the Bible's stories literally true? What can I believe? Does my life have value? Is there forgiveness? Is there any hope? These are the questions Liberal Christianity must answer. It is to this multicultural, multiracial and secular world that we must speak.

For the past 25 years I have searched for a book that laid out simply and clearly what liberal Christians believe and what Mainline churches should do. Unable to find it, I finally decided to write it myself. What follows is the result.

James Albert Flurer
Christmas Day 1993
Berks County, Pennsylvania

Chapter 1

TEMPLES STILL UNDONE

A Turning Point

We live at a pivotal time in human history. Not since the turn of the last millennium has the future been filled with such promise and danger.

As the year 1000 A.D. approached, Christian Europe was threatened on every side. Viking raiders swept out of the north to attack Europe's coastal cities. From the east came the Magyars pushing toward Germany, Italy and France. Most threatening of all, the sword of Islam had come thundering out of the Arabian deserts, captured the Holy Lands, conquered North Africa and seized half Portugal and Spain. It seemed the inevitable collapse of Europe and Christianity was near.

During this period, the church had been standing guard over the West's spiritual traditions for nearly 500 years. As the Roman Empire's political structures crumbled and barbarian invasions threatened, the church withdrew into monastic communities that could be maintained independent of the outside world. Both church and monastery buildings looked like fortresses designed to protect and defend. Behind thick rock walls, monks engaged in reading, writing and resolutely copying ancient texts by hand. Centuries of Western knowledge and wisdom hung by this fragile thread.

But fresh winds were blowing. The new millennium's arrival did not mark the end, but a turning point. Suddenly, a creative burst of spiritual energy swept the continent.

In 1144 near Paris, an event occurred symbolic of the transformation taking place. In June of that year, Abbot Suger consecrated his newly rebuilt cathedral of Saint-Denis, traditional burial place of French kings. The country's elite who attended were stunned by what they saw. The vast open spaces, the graceful pointed arches, the glorious windows. From that moment, the influence of Suger's wondrous new style began to spread; first in France; then across the continent. The age of the Gothic cathedral had begun.

Over the next two hundred years, Western Europe was crowned with a garland of churches unlike any built before. At Paris, Chartres, Canterbury, Amiens, Cologne, elegant slender columns replaced heavy stone pillars. Massive walls became glass curtains that transformed the interior space with shimmering colored light. Towering spires and vaulted ceilings reached ever higher. Unlike those of the past, these churches were not fortresses. They were outposts of heaven.

The spiritual power that built the Gothic cathedrals inspired more than architecture. Economic life rebounded. Trade flourished. Education blossomed. The great universities opened their doors at Oxford, Padua and Paris. Scholars like Thomas Aquinas focused their considerable intellects on the timeless questions of Christian faith. Within the church, old religious orders were reformed and new ones founded.

Europe was being remade.

PROMISE AND DANGER

Now, as the year 2000 approaches, we stand again at the threshold of just such a decisive moment, not just for Europe, but for the world. Obviously, it cannot be proved that such a spiritual flowering will occur but that critical years lie ahead, no one can doubt. Even a quick glance at the world scene makes that evident.

Modern technology has expanded human power beyond the cathedral maker's wildest dreams. For example, the main tower at Chartres pushed 30 stories above the French countryside. Today, it is technically possible to build a skyscraper three miles high. Satellites and space shuttles circle the earth. Atomic power heats our morning coffee and could, of course, end all life on earth.

The communications and transportation revolution has created what we now call the global village. For example, John Nisbitt points out in *Megatrends* that when John Wilkes Booth shot Abraham Lincoln in 1865, the news took five days to reach London. When the assassination attempt on Ronald Reagan's life occurred in 1981, a British reporter was working within a block of the hotel where the shooting took place. He learned about it minutes later when his editor in London called on the telephone. His editor had seen the attack on British television.

Advances grow exponentially. In 1910, my maternal grandfather came to the United States from the Caribbean island of Barbados on a ship powered by sails. Before he died, he had seen us put a man in space. What advances will we see? Our children? Our grandchildren?

Enormous forces press humanity to think and act globally. Pesticides sprayed in Kansas end up in the fat cells of Arctic polar bears. Trees cut down in Brazil's rain forests impact the corn harvest in Pennsylvania. The whole world is learning the truth of John Donne's poetic principle that no one is an island.

Although modern technology can be used for good or ill, some modern forces are truly malevolent. For example, the Swiss psychologist Carl Jung wrote that during the 20th century the Western world went through a kind of schizophrenic split symbolized by the Iron Curtain. Those of us living in the West projected our evil upon those on the other side. "We are not the ones with evil intentions," we said. "Those to be feared and hated are the atheistic communists and their fellow travelers."

In the East, the situation was reversed. Like us, they believed their intentions were pure. It was the hated imperialists and their running dogs who were humankind's real enemies.

In 1956, Jung could not foresee the Iron Curtain's crumbling but the results of communism's fall are becoming painfully clear. In Matthew's gospel, Jesus tells a story that sheds light on the situation.

> *When an evil spirit comes out of a man, it goes through arid places seeking rest and does not find it. Then it says, "I will return to the house I left." When it arrives, it finds the house unoccupied, swept clean and put in order. Then it goes and takes with it seven other spirits more wicked than itself, and they go in and live there. And the final condition of that man is worse than the first. That is how it will be with this wicked generation (Matthew 12:43-45 NIV).*

How will it be with our own "wicked generation"? Like the demons in Jesus' story, communism's collapse has freed dark, powerful psychic forces to roam the world. The "enemy" across the Iron Curtain allowed each side to avoid facing their own inner demons, that is, their potential for evil and their fear of that potential. Now we must all either face the truth about ourselves or find new enemies to fear and hate.

The morning headlines make the situation clear. The demons are coming home with a vengeance. We are finding new enemies. Hate, resentment and anger become ever more rampant between races, religions and national groups. Nor are political opponents immune from hostility's rising tide. From Eastern Europe to the American abortion debate, the prophet's injunction, "Come let us reason together . . ." is swept aside.

Saint Paul was correct. Our struggle is not against enemies of flesh and blood but against "the cosmic powers of this present darkness." These menacing psychic forces that move outside humanity's conscious control add a profound element of uncertainty and danger to the world situation.

Who can deny the dangers and opportunities that lie ahead? Enormous power rests in human hands. It is within our grasp to advance human life toward untold blessings or to realize the Medieval age's most fearful nightmare, that the Book of Revelation's prophecy might come true. That the world would end in one, great terrible apocalypse.

WHO'S VISION WILL SHAPE THE FUTURE?

Who's vision will guide the powerful forces now shaping the future? Will we be dominated by merchants of greed who seek instant profits and immediate gratification despite future costs? Will we create an ever widening gulf between rich and poor both in America and the world? Will we leave a legacy of poisoned air, undrinkable water, contaminated soil, global warming and flooded coastlines? Will we transform the planet into a global wasteland?

Will the future be ruled by machine men, like Darth Vader of the Star Wars saga? Will we use our technology to serve human ends or crush our humanity? Will we again unleash the atomic bomb's fearsome power? Will our civilization be remembered only for its terrifying laser guided missiles and 13-year-old terrorists with high tech assault rifles? That is, of course, if anyone is left to remember us at all.

Will authoritarian religious or political forces seize control? Will governments akin to Iran's sweep the world under the banner of "God, authority and fatherland?" Will a counterrevolution based on religious fundamentalism or on an aristocracy of wealth and privilege turn back the ideals of freedom, human dignity and the common good?

Or perhaps we will be seduced by the materialism of Madison Avenue and its counterparts around the globe. One of my colleagues tells about hosting an Amish family for dinner. The Amish are a small religious sect with many living near my home in southern Pennsylvania's rolling hills. Distinct because they reject the modern world, the Amish use no electricity, own no cars, no televisions, no dishwashers. They choose to live as if it were still the 18th century.

After dinner, as my colleague and his wife cleared the table, their teenage children and Amish friends left the kitchen. Soon squeals of laughter were coming from the living room. Looking around the corner, my friend saw his son teaching the Amish children to play Nintendo video games. Their parents, people who radically reject the modern world, could not help but laugh with them.

The modern world is seductive indeed.

The Future's Architects

What will the future bring? Who will be its architects? Who will chart its course? I suggest Liberal Christianity can and must provide the blueprint to move the world's life forward.

But before we go any further, let me be clear. By "Liberal Christianity" I mean that broad movement within the church working to make Christianity's essential message relevant and compelling for the modern world.

As we will see in Chapter 2, Medieval Christianity taught the earth was flat and did not move. It believed "man" was creation's capstone. It saw a world filled with a multitude of angels, demons and supernatural events. It taught that God was in his heaven, not far beyond the moon, watching over his creation to reward the good and punish the wicked.

But the modern world's rise over the past 500 years has shattered these traditional assumptions. Two developments, science and secularization, are primarily responsible for this crisis. Science has proved its methods are the most reliable guide to practical truth. Secularization has meant that life here and now is more important than the life of the world to come. Together, these forces have profoundly shaken Medieval Christianity's most basic convictions about human life, the universe and God.

Rather than stand by and watch Christianity's eventual collapse, the liberal tradition took up the challenge to rebuild and reinterpret the Christian vision. Simply put, liberalism's goal is to reconstruct Christianity for the modern world.

Like our spiritual ancestors who fashioned Sainte-Chapelle's magnificent windows and built Chartres' towering spires, liberal Christians must now help guide the modern world's forces. We must provide the vision for the future's builders and be catalysts that move the world toward spiritual values, humane uses of technology and ecological sanity. There are new cathedrals to be raised, not with mortar, glass and stone, but with clear thought, passionate commitment and decisive action.

THE TASK AHEAD

In response to John the Baptist's preaching, the crowds asked, "What then must we do?" That is a critical question for the liberal church today. I suggest we face three key tasks. They involve: message, community and mission.

A Clear Message

First, we must state liberal Christian beliefs clearly, simply and persuasively. Liberals argue Christianity's essential message of a loving God is compatible with modern science and is still profoundly true, relevant and, in fact, crucial to modern men and women. Yet to convince modern people of Christianity's truths, we must, at the very least, be able to state what we believe those truths to be.

How many times have even long-time church members asked, "What does our church believe? The fundamentalists are so clear and certain. Why do I feel so confused?" Too often the answer is, "Well, we let people make up their own minds." Or, "In our church, we believe in social service and social action."

Clearly, that is not enough.

True, liberal Christians believe in individual conscience before God. We do make up our own minds. We owe our conscience to neither king nor clergy, but to God alone. However, in making up our minds, we learn from tradition, the Bible and each other. We struggle together to extend our common understanding of Christianity's great issues.

And yes, the well-being of people does concern us, a concern acted out in both deeds of personal kindness and organized political action. But we are not the Sierra Club, Planned Parenthood nor even the Democratic Party at prayer. The church lives by every word that comes from the mouth of God, not the words published by sociologists, psychiatrists nor politicians no matter how wise and well intentioned they may be.

Central to the church is what James Joyce called the "grave and constant" in human life: the mystery of God and existence, pain and suffering, good and evil, life and death. These issues will not be solved by any social agenda.

The ancient church father's task was to explain Christianity to the Roman world. The liberal task has been to make it understandable to the modern world. That remains our task today.

A Caring Community

Second, local churches must be places of refuge, encouragement and renewal. We must be communities dedicated to the cure of souls. Let me give you an example of what I mean.

A few years ago, I attended a meeting on a warm spring evening held at a church near my home. Arriving, I was shocked that I could not find a parking space in this quiet suburban neighborhood. The streets were lined with cars.

Nearly 100 people were milling around, obviously waiting for some sort of meeting at the church to begin. Some were expensively dressed men and women in their 40's and 50's. Others were young people with rock-and-roll T-shirts, ripped jeans and every description of dress in between. Vehicles ranged from BMW's to motorcycles.

I could not imagine what church event could draw such a wide ranging group in class, age and dress. I asked a church member what had brought all these people there on a Wednesday night. His answer: "Alcoholics Anonymous."

I have asked friends and colleagues who attend AA what these meetings mean to them. They say Alcoholics Anonymous gives them a chance to tell the truth about themselves and see forgiveness in other's eyes. A chance to be accepted and to be challenged when they are wrong. A chance to help other people and make a difference in the world.

Can our churches do less?

A Compelling Mission

Third, the church must be a moral authority for change. Our mission is nothing less than the world's transformation, that God's will be done on earth as it is in heaven.

In what may be an apocryphal story, it is said that when Harry Emerson Fosdick became the first pastor of New York City's Riverside Church, he stood in the pulpit for his inaugural sermon as the city's elite crowded the pews. For a few moments Fosdick gazed around the sanctuary built by Rockefeller millions. Then he began his message with these words: "It is strange to remember that all of this is built in honor of a Galilean carpenter who had no place to lay his head." Strange, indeed. If the story isn't true, it should be.

The church is not a social service agency, but neither are we a country club with stained glass windows. Christ did not suffer the cross' agonies so that nice people could meet Sunday morning over sermons and coffee. Christ lived and died so the blind might see, the lame walk, the deaf hear, the dead be raised to life and the poor hear good news.

I remember meeting a young "Moonie" disciple during a layover at the Newark airport some years ago. As we spoke I wondered what motivated this middle class graduate of a famous eastern university with a traditional mainline church upbringing. Why had she given up a promising career on Madison Avenue and her religious heritage to join the Moonies? She explained that her parents told her to get a good education, a good job and marry well. But she wanted to help Rev. Moon save the world.

Evidently, this young woman did not think her home church was particularly interested in saving the world. Or, if it was, it did not need her help. Correct or incorrect, these perceptions of the liberal church must change and soon.

WHERE DO WE GO FROM HERE?

The remainder of this book explores the liberal Christian tradition, its past, present and future. We begin in Chapter 2 by surveying the modern world's rise and analyze its challenge to the Medieval church's vision. We examine how the Renaissance, Reformation and science, as well as modern political, industrial and technological revolutions have shattered traditional Christianity's most basic assumptions.

We focus specifically on modern science in Chapter 3 and consider the turmoil it has created for faith. Reviewing Newton, Darwin and the advances since, we find that science now believes it can account for the universe without speaking about meaning, values or a living God. Conservatives within the church have fought a continuing and fruitless rear guard action trying to stem science's advance. In contrast, liberals, both Catholic and Protestant, have welcomed scientific progress, arguing that science and Christianity are compatible. Each has its own arena. It is possible to accept and use science's findings, enjoy technology's advances and still be a committed Christian.

Yet even if science's challenge can be met, another difficult hurdle must be overcome: the mystery of evil and suffering. In Chapter 4, we ask, "Why do the innocent suffer?" Besides the traditional Christian answer, we explore another possibility. Suffering exists because, although divine love is infinite, divine power is not. God would end suffering immediately, yet something within the very "stuff" of existence makes that impossible. This view portrays a suffering, crucified God who struggles with suffering humanity to reach divine goals.

Chapter 5 examines the liberal understanding of the Bible. Neither God's literal words, nor just any book, the Bible reveals the living God. Yet because it was written in a prescientific age, liberals understand its supernatural, mythic stories must be interpreted symbolically. Further, not all scripture is of equal value. Most important are the gospel's stories of the cross and resurrection. They reveal more clearly than anywhere else God's suffering love for the world and provide the standard by which all beliefs and moral actions must be judged.

Chapter 6 lays out the tradition of liberal belief. We examine its design principles, its four pillars, and the stone and mortar with which it builds. We look in detail at beliefs like freedom and responsibility, individual conscience, human nature, the social gospel, human dignity, moral behavior, tolerance, democratic government and the possibility of progress.

The spiritual life is the topic of Chapter 7. Here, Liberal Christianity has been weak but this need not be so. A promising future can be found with the 12 Step movement now proving so powerful in recovery groups around the world.

In fact, 12 Steps began as the Christian Oxford movement's 8 Points. In the 1930s, Alcoholics Anonymous adapted it for its purposes. The principles behind the 8 Points and the 12 Steps offer both a dynamic and reasonable approach to spiritual life that can be revived by the liberal church.

In Chapter 8, we see how the liberal Christian vision can and must become the inspiration behind Mainline church renewal. Analyzing the human needs that lie outside our walls, we look at how local congregations can be beacons of hope, comfort and challenge to our communities and our world. Finally, we confront some of the critical choices Mainline churches must face in the years ahead.

But what has happened over the past 500 years that has left the Christian world so shaken? What developments changed the way we view the world, ourselves, our lives and our God? It is to these questions we now turn.

Chapter 2

O'ER CRUMBLING WALLS

From Abbot Suger To Hiroshima

Like other Christians during the Gothic age, Abbot Suger, Saint-Denis' builder, undoubtedly lived with the pious confidence that God was in his heaven and all was right with the world. The church spoke with divine authority. The pope, standing in St. Peter's line of succession, was Christ's vicar on earth. Following the Biblical tradition begun by King Saul and the prophet Samuel, kings were anointed by the church and wielded the government's sword by divine right. To oppose the king's authority meant opposing the authority of God himself.

The Medieval Age still viewed the world much like the biblical writers. Both believed it was akin to a three-layer cake, with heaven "up there" where God reigned on his majestic throne. The earth was in the middle, and hell was down below where the wicked were punished.

It was a neat, orderly universe. From street urchin to king, everyone in Medieval society understood their role in the divine scheme and found security in it. Humankind looked eagerly upward to God and heaven. In heaven, they would receive both compensation for life's hardships and reward for virtue's deeds.

MICHELANGELO'S DAVID AND THE RENAISSANCE

But as the sun rose over Florence, Italy, on the morning of May 14, 1504, things were changing. Michelangelo had finished his statue of David and it was being moved from the Florence cathedral workshop to the Palazzo Vecchio. Here, it would take its place of honor as the city's symbol.

Originally, Florence's leaders had hired Michelangelo's genius to carve the statue for their cathedral. But when the city's leaders saw it, they decided to enshrine the 14 foot tall masterpiece in front of the town hall.

Colossal in size, nothing like it had been carved in the West since antiquity. This was not, however, the Bible's vision of a slight, teenaged shepherd boy. Beautiful, elegant, powerfully muscular, Michelangelo's David represented more than 16th century Florence's refinement and influence. It symbolized the beginning of the modern spirit. Attention was turning from the heavens and God's mighty acts, to the earth and man's noble deeds. Here was the doctrine of man's perfectibility chiseled in marble.

The cathedral at Saint-Denis probably did not feel the ground tremble as Florence's colossus was finally lowered into place. But just 17 years later an event would occur whose shock waves would be felt at Saint-Denis and far beyond.

LUTHER AND THE REFORMATION

In 1521, Martin Luther (1483-1546) was summoned to

defend himself at the Diet of Worms. He was charged with rejecting theology based on tradition, opposition to the sale of indulgences and his refusal to accept both the pope's supremacy and the infallibility of the general councils. It was at Worms he gave his legendary response, "Here I stand, I can do no other. God help me."

Although scholars debate whether Luther actually concluded with those dramatic words, the point was clear. Depending on nothing but his conscience and interpretation of scripture, an unknown German monk had challenged both the pope and the emperor's authority and lived to tell about it. He did, of course, have the protection of a few German princes who sometimes seemed more interested in political schemes than the salvation of immortal souls.

Nevertheless, Luther's refusal to recant stirred the European pot of discontent that was already bubbling. Heading home from Worms, Luther fell into the hands of friendly kidnappers. They whisked him away to Wartburg Castle, safe from the imperial ban that had been declared against him. From Wartburg he continued his struggle.

In 1522, Luther began translating the New Testament into German. Until that point, the Bible had been primarily available in Latin. The average person never read it and knew little about what it contained. It was the church's job to read and interpret; the faithful's job was to believe.

Luther, however, wanted the Bible available to all. Apparently, he felt that once everyone could read the Bible for themselves, they would agree with him against the pope. Five hundred denominations later, we know there is more than one or two or a hundred ways to interpret the Bible.

Luther and his fellow reformers raised the banner of "Sola Scriptura," or "scripture alone." By this they meant scripture should be the only authority and the sole test of faith. At Worms he said that if he could be proved wrong by scripture, he would recant, but only then. Luther believed he was establishing the Bible as authority's new keystone. In fact, he had set in motion a process that would shatter the church's authority and, eventually, the Bible's authority as well.

Soon preachers were springing up all over Europe with new biblical interpretations. The church split and split again. First into Catholics and Lutherans. Then Zwinglians were added, then Calvinists, then Anglicans, then Anabaptists.

Who really knew the truth? Where did authority really lie? Where was it all going to end? This time, Saint Denis undoubtedly felt the tremors coming from Germany but it could not possibly have been prepared for what was to come next.

COPERNICUS: IT MOVES

Almost 400 years after Abbot Suger had consecrated Saint-Denis, in 1543 a Polish scholar from Frauenburg published a new book. His name was Copernicus (1473-1543). The book was entitled *On the Revolutions of the Heavenly Spheres* and it would soon rattle Saint-Denis' windows and shake its walls.

As we have seen, the biblical writers and the Medieval church both believed in a world picture that developed about 5,000 B.C. in the Near East. The world was like a three-layer cake. Above the earth, supported by huge "pillars of the sky," was a ceiling or canopy known as the firmament (literally, from the original Hebrew, a strip of metal). Above the firmament were the storehouses for the rain, hail and a chamber for the wind. Finally came the "highest heaven" where God reigned.

Down below were the "pillars of the earth," and sheol, the place of the dead. Over time, sheol would become the location of hell where the wicked were punished and purgatory where souls were chastened until fit for heaven.

But there was one central idea so important that it almost became church dogma. Both the biblical writers and the

Medieval church believed the earth was flat and immovable as anyone could plainly tell. After all, did not the psalmist say, "He set the earth on its foundations; it can never be moved" (Psalm 104:5 NIV). In this conception, the sun and stars revolved around the earth. The earth was the center of the universe and man was creation's capstone.

But Copernicus showed it was not true! The psalmist was wrong! The earth was not flat but a sphere. And, it moved!

What did it all mean? If the earth was not the universe's center, did that also mean man was not creation's capstone? If the earth revolved around the sun, where was "up there"? If God was not "up there" looking down over his flock to reward the good and punish the wicked, where was he and what was he doing? Still worse, and most disturbing, if the church had been wrong about this, about what else might it also be wrong?

Ironically, *On the Revolutions* was dedicated to Pope Paul III and its printing was paid for and supervised by German Protestants. Its implications, however, would soon become too frightful to contemplate. In years to come, scholars like Galileo would suggest such ideas only at the risk of imprisonment, torture and death. And, in the church's eyes, eternal damnation as well.

POLITICAL REVOLUTION

As if this had not been enough, another clash followed. This time the target was political authority.

Christendom's kings ruled by the principle of divine right that could be traced back to the Bible. In the Book of 1 Samuel we learn that the people of Israel wanted a king so they could be like the surrounding nations. God reluctantly agreed and selected Saul to rule and the prophet Samuel to anoint him king. By God's authority, Saul would govern as long as he followed divine commands. Following a parallel to the Bible, the church anointed Medieval European kings who ruled "by the grace of God." Their governing power still rested, at least in theory, upon divine right.

In 1776, however, America's founding fathers saw things differently. "We hold these truths to be self-evident," wrote Thomas Jefferson, "that all men are created equal, that they are endowed by their Creator with certain unalienable Rights. That among these are Life, Liberty, and the pursuit of Happiness."

So, the king did not rule by divine right after all. The government's just powers derived from the consent of the governed, not from noble birth or anointing by the church. God gave rights to the people, not the king.

The American Revolution was a polite affair compared with what followed in France. Not only did the French reject their king's divine right to rule, they cut off his head. In contrast to the Old Testament's David who refused to raise his hand against the Lord's anointed, the French revolutionary government was only too eager to send King Louis XVI for a bloody appointment with Dr. Guillotine's invention.

In 1804, the scene shifted to Notre Dame cathedral. Napoleon Bonaparte, the revolution's "First Consul for life," had been declared emperor by the Senate. And, because an emperor could hardly be crowned without a pope on hand, the aging and infirm Pius VII made the long, difficult journey to Paris. He would be present to place the imperial crown on Napoleon's head.

Finally on December 2, Napoleon entered the great cathedral and approached Pius VII who held the golden crown on a red velvet cushion. Taking the crown from the pope, he turned his back to face the crowd and placed it on his head, thus becoming Napoleon I, Emperor of the French.

Napoleon took the crown to make it clear he had become emperor by the people's will, not the pope's grace. From that moment, Europe's monarchs were his sworn enemies. With that kind of thinking, no king's head was safe.

Europe's hereditary rulers staged a counterattack. They swore not to lay down the sword until the "troublemaker of Europe" was driven from the throne and hopefully from this life. For the next ten years, almost without pause, the battle raged from Lisbon on the Atlantic to the gates of Moscow. Finally, after his defeat at Waterloo, Napoleon went off to exile on the South Atlantic island of St. Helena and the French kings returned to the throne. But the die was cast.

After the American and French revolutions, government based on noble birth, divine right and church authority was finished. No crowned head could sleep peacefully until they had turned over their power to a constitutional government. The old aristocracy's banner, "God, King and Fatherland," was coming down. The modern world's tricolor was rising. It read: "Liberty, Equality and Fraternity."

Abbot Suger's successor at Saint-Denis must have shaken his head in wonder and shame. When even the Lord's own anointed king was no longer safe from his own people, what in the world was happening?

INDUSTRIAL REVOLUTION

What in fact was happening was a dramatic rise in living standards. From biblical times until the Middle Ages, life had changed very little. Humanity struggled day by day to scratch out an existence from the earth much as it had done for two thousand years. Life was hard, brutish and short. People looked for the comfort of heavenly rewards; for most, there was no place else to look.

The industrial revolution changed all that. Although it had been developing for hundreds of years, after 1840 the pace quickened. New factories and machine-made products produced material wealth that would have astounded the Medieval world. In 1144 at Saint-Denis' consecration, even the king could not arrive by car, enjoy air conditioning or watch television.

The assembly line, mass production and a questing modern spirit were changing everything. People like Henry Ford, Alexander Graham Bell, Thomas Edison, the Wright brothers and Andrew Carnegie were remaking the world, not in God's image, but in man's.

When humanity discovered it need not wait for heaven's comforts, men and women became increasingly interested in this world and less interested in the next. Humanity stopped looking up and began looking forward, to the newest technological advance and the latest modern convenience.

And what about Saint-Denis? It was still beautiful, a great vacation spot. The faith it represented was not really that objectionable, just increasingly irrelevant. There seemed no point in waiting for "pie in the sky" because pie, and much else, could be had right here and now.

HIROSHIMA: THE END

Finally, on the morning of August 6, 1945, an American B-29 bomber called the Enola Gay took off from its Pacific Island base and headed for Japan. World War II was nearing its end. Germany had already surrendered unconditionally and now Japan would be forced to surrender. Within the plane's bomb bay was a single atomic bomb, code name, Little Boy.

Imagine for a moment that Abbot Suger's Saint-Denis, that beautiful little Gothic gem, was located, not on the outskirts of Paris, but on the outskirts of Hiroshima. Visualize in your mind's eye the first brilliant millisecond of atomic light, a thousand times brighter than the sun. Picture the first shock wave as it hits the cathedral, blasting its glorious windows into a hundred billion shards of sparkling colored glass. Imagine as the graceful vaulted ceiling cracks and huge chunks begin to fall, as the beautiful columns start collapsing and the tower begins crashing to earth.

Modern humanity had done the unimaginable. The builders of the Tower of Babel had tried to reach heaven and failed. Luther and Napoleon had only defied God's representatives on earth. But the scientists who built that first atomic bomb had reached up into heaven and seized divine prerogatives. They had taken into mortal hands power previously reserved to God alone. Power to smite cities. To shatter civilizations. To destroy the world.

The old certain faith had come to an end. With Nazi death camps like Auschwitz and Dachau where bodies were stacked like cord wood and with that single flash of light over Hiroshima, Abbot Suger's Medieval Christian vision was finished. Could it be that God was still in his heaven and all was right with the world? Could it be the God who noted even the sparrow's fall still reigned on high? Now, or so it appeared to many, God was dead and the world lay in ruins.

SUMMARY

In this chapter we have examined the modern world's rise spanning 500 years from Michelangelo's David to Hiroshima's destruction.

We have seen the change in how modern men and women understand and value the world and themselves. Modern people accept science's methods; they make sense and they work. We accept that the earth is one of many planets rotating around a star, part of a vast universe. We believe in democracy's virtues and the individual's rights against the coercive power of the state and mass society. We enjoy cars, central heating, elevators and all the rest that modern technology provides. We take pride in human accomplishment. We thrill at the sight of the space shuttle's engines roaring to life even as we fear the possibility of nuclear and ecological destruction.

Yet, as different as our understanding of the world may be, biologically, we are exactly the same as our Medieval cousins. We still have two eyes, two arms, two lungs, one heart, one brain. We are born, grow up, reach maturity, grow old and die.

The same questions that confronted my ancestor, Michael Flurer, born 1689, Adolzhausen, Germany, confront me, born 1947, Darby, Pennsylvania, USA. We are still confronted by the mystery of existence: Where am I and where am I going? What is the purpose of my being here? We remain challenged by ethic's demands: What is the good and should be done? What is evil and should be avoided? We are still puzzled by questions of identity: Who am I and how do I live a good human life in this time and place?

Medieval Christianity is dead but Christianity is not. Can liberals explain Christianity's essential message to the people of this new, chaotic, seductive, dangerous, many-splendored world? Can the broken stone be raised? In the next chapter we turn our attention to those tasks.

Chapter 3

RAISE THE BROKEN STONE

The Challenge Of Modern Science

We have seen how the forces unleashed by the modern world's rise have undercut Christianity, yet no force has had a greater impact than modern science. Today, no religious viewpoint can be taken seriously that does not take into account science's role in the world.

Therefore, in this chapter we examine modern science and its influence. First, we find that science, not faith, has become the most reliable guide to practical truth for modern men and women. Second, we consider Sir Isaac Newton's universe machine and Darwin's theory of evolution. Taken together and including advances since, science now believes it can account for the universe without speaking of purpose, meaning, values, or the Christian idea of a loving God.

We also review Christianity's response. We see that conservatives have struggled against scientific progress: first, by discouraging research, and second, by attacking and ridiculing its results.

Liberal Christianity takes a different approach. Liberals contend that science and religion are compatible. Each has its proper arena. The facts presented by science can be understood in ways that support faith and the Christian vision. Further, as the 3rd century church father Origen suggested, all the world's learning can be used and useful in building the Lord's temple. This is especially true of Carl Jung's depth psychology. The broken stone can be raised.

Modern Science: Guide To Practical Truth

In the Medieval world, there was one source of truth: the church and its authority. If the church said the sun revolved around the earth, then it was so, despite what Galileo said he saw through his telescope.

Even the humble vacuum tube became involved in controversy. In 1643, Evangelista Torricelli (1608-1647), one of Galileo's former assistants and a professor of mathematics in Florence, argued that atmospheric pressure did exist and a vacuum could be created. Using a glass tube filled with mercury and closed at one end, Torricelli covered the open end with his finger and placed it in a dish of mercury. Removing his finger, the mercury in the tube fell, creating a vacuum at the closed end. He had succeeded in making a primitive barometer that registered atmospheric pressure and he had created a vacuum.

Unfortunately, this was exactly what the church said could not be done. Following ideas expressed by Aristotle, church scholars said a vacuum could not exist and forbade further experiments. Torricelli was forced to send his notes across the border to France in order for experimentation to continue.

For modern men and women, this kind of demand for blind faith in direct opposition to the facts is intolerable. Instead, moderns look to the scientific method based on experimentation, observation and conclusions that can be tested. We want to believe what we know and know what we believe.

Clearly, science has become the most reliable guide to practical truth for the modern world. Its methods work and have paid handsome dividends in knowledge, comfort and increased life spans.

A WORLD WITHOUT GOD

Newton And The Universe Machine

Science has also dramatically affected how modern people picture the world. In 1687, Isaac Newton (1642-1727) published *Principa Mathematica*, or *Mathematical Principles*. Here, Newton pictured a vast universe machine that worked according to natural laws that could be studied and discovered. Unlike the Medieval world in which God moved the sun and stars and regularly intervened in human affairs, Newton's universe operated in a reliable and predictable way. God had designed the machine, built it, started it up, and then let it run.

Was there any need for God in this new universe? Newton thought there was. A religious man who studied both science and theology, he saw what he thought were irregularities in the orbits of the planets. Newton assumed that every so often God needed to correct these slight deviations to keep everything running smoothly.

The God Of The Gaps

Yet, Newton's assumption, and others like it, soon proved unsatisfactory to both science and religion. Such arguments became known as "the God of the Gaps." For example, picture Sir Isaac at his desk working out a long complex mathematical formula. Finally, baffled about how to proceed, he writes, "And then a miracle occurs!" In short, when science could not provide the answer with its own methods, God would be rushed in to fill the gap.

However, the astronomer Pierre Laplace (1749-1827) eventually solved Newton's problem. It turned out God was not needed to adjust the planets after all.

The implications were clear. As science pushed forward, God would be forced to ever more remote corners of the universe until there was no room left for divine action. Science would advance until everything that could be known, was known.

But what did science want to know? Science's methods work best with things that can be observed by the senses, measured, and expressed in mathematical terms. It wants to know size, shape, mass, velocity, physical composition and material relationships. It was a short step to the idea that anything that cannot be known by science's methods cannot be known at all, and therefore, is not real.

Eventually, Newton's universe machine would not need God's help to make it run. Perhaps, it did not need any God at all.

Darwin And The Theory Of Evolution

No one has had a greater impact on modern thought than Charles Darwin (1809-1882). The fields of biology, psychology, history, economics, political science, philosophy and religion have all felt his theory's impact. All have used his language. All have used his idea that life evolves.

Born at Shrewsbury, England, in 1809, Darwin began his studies at Edinburgh to become a doctor like his father.

However, his lackluster performance soon proved he was not really interested in medicine. Next, his father encouraged him to consider a vocation as a country pastor. Darwin found the idea appealing and went off to Cambridge to study for the ministry. Again, his performance proved his disinterest. Eventually, he followed his real love: science.

From 1831 until 1836, he made his famous voyage aboard the H.M.S. *Beagle* as naturalist on a South American surveying expedition. During his journey, the differences between animals on the mainland and nearby islands impressed him. Comparing living animals with fossil remains in the area, he discovered that although closely related, they were not the same. He wondered how species of plants and animals changed and concluded that these differences "could only be explained on the supposition that species gradually become modified."

In 1859, Darwin's classic work *The Origin of Species* appeared explaining his theory of evolution. Briefly stated, he believed that life evolved over time through a process of natural selection based on the struggle for existence, random variation and the survival of the fittest.

Contrary to the first chapter of Genesis which tells how God created the earth in six days, Darwin argued that life evolved over millions of years by a natural mechanical process. Humanity was not creation's capstone nor made by a special act of creation. According to evolution, the same process that created humans also created worms, tadpoles and beetles.

Fittingly, when Darwin died on April 19, 1882, he was buried in Westminster Abbey — next to Sir Isaac Newton. Together, they shook the Christian world. Newton's universe machine removed the need for God's intervention in the working of nature. Darwin shook the belief that humans were divinely created, a little lower than the angels and in the image of God.

Science's World Picture

Clearly, great advances have taken place since Newton and Darwin. Scientists no longer talk of a universe machine but about relativity, black holes and quarks. Beginning with Newton and Darwin and adding advances since, science confronts us with a world picture that is grim indeed.

Billions of years ago, all the matter of the visible universe was so dense and tightly compressed that it was smaller than a human fingertip. Then a huge explosion occurred: The Big Bang. The universe began rapidly expanding and over billions of years evolved into the multitude of stars, planets and galaxies that exist today. The earth is an infinitesimal speck in the vast ocean of space and, like all the universe, is eventually headed for cosmic death.

Further, millions of years ago on earth a single or a few pools of chemical stew happened to contain the necessary building blocks for organic life. A random lightning strike started the process that created all the living things we now see on earth. Additionally, it all happened by chance and might never have happened at all.

In any case, humans are no more than sophisticated monkeys. The mental processes that allow us to think, reason, feel emotion, develop personality and experience a sense of personal identity are nothing more than extremely intricate chemical reactions in the brain.

A completely natural mechanical process has created human beings. The universe has made us, but is neither aware of it, nor does it care. It is like a computer assembling automobile air bag devices. Perhaps to the naive or superstitious, it may appear the computer is acting on a deep sympathy for human well being, but it is not so.

To sum up, God is non-existent. The human quest for salvation and meaning is a fantasy designed to make up for the wretchedness of our true situation. We have been cast up upon the shore of a far corner of the universe and are on our own to make of life what we can. We are alone in the universe. And like all living creatures, and the universe itself, we will die.

CHRISTIANITY RESPONDS

When we last left Saint-Denis, our symbol for Medieval faith, we imagined it on the outskirts of Hiroshima, a ruined pile of shattered glass and broken stone. Clearly, nothing in science's world picture offers much encouragement for its rebuilding.

Many were deeply shaken as the old certainties came crashing down, one after another. John Donne wrote that everything was "in pieces, all coherence gone." The French mathematician Blaise Pascal spoke for many when he confessed "the eternal silence of the infinite spaces" frightened him.

Yet, where some saw danger and destruction, others saw dazzling possibilities. Many were awed that God could create so vast and magnificent a universe. Others thought it marvelous that God was bringing about such deep and extraordinary changes as time went by and wondered what glories might still be to come.

A Question Of Authority

The real issue for Christianity was the question of authority. Who really knew the right questions to ask? Who really knew the answers? Who really knew the truth?

For Rome's conservative followers, authority was found in the church and its teachings. The church knew the questions, the answers, the truth. If it was shown it did not, the whole edifice would come crashing down or at best survive as an empty shell.

The same principle held true for conservative Protestants who believed the Bible was God's inerrant, authoritative word. If errors or contradictions were found, however small, the game was lost.

For conservative Christians, then, there was no choice. Any scientific advance that contradicted the church or the Bible's teaching had to be opposed and defeated. No concessions could be made because the first concession, conceded all. Once the church or Bible was shown to be wrong anywhere, it undermined their authority everywhere.

The battle was fierce but terribly lopsided. When it came to examining and analyzing the physical world, science was in its element. The church was not.

Galileo

Let us examine two examples. In 1611, Galileo (1564-1642) arrived in Rome with his new telescope hoping to dazzle the pope's court and he did. Encouraged by his warm reception, he felt free to express strong opinions on the new Copernican system and even attempted to prove it was scriptural. When a warning in 1615 did not discourage him, Pope Paul V told him directly not to "hold, teach, or defend" this new scientific doctrine.

Returning to Florence, Galileo continued his work and again ran afoul of the church. Summoned to Rome by the Inquisition, he pleaded that ill health and old age prevented him from coming, but no excuse was tolerated. Arriving in Rome in 1633, he was examined under threat of torture, although it was never carried out and, perhaps, never seriously intended. Finally realizing the gravity of his situation, Galileo recanted. Allowed to leave Rome, eventually he returned to Florence where he spent the remainder of his life under house arrest.

Clearly grasping the stakes, the church tried to prevent scientific research from taking place and its findings from spreading. In Galileo's case, they succeeded but the scientific tide was rising and would soon prove impossible to stop.

The Scopes Monkey Trial

The conservative Protestant church had no better luck. In 1859, the publication of Darwin's *Origins* hit the scene like a hurricane. Samuel Wilberforce, bishop of Oxford, unleashed a sarcastic torrent against the new theory. Revivalist Billy Sunday condemned it as "the bastard theory of evolution." But sarcasm and ridicule were no more successful in blunting science's growing momentum than Roman threats.

In 1925, the battle moved to an American court room in Dayton, Tennessee. Here, state law forbad "the teaching of the evolution theory in all universities, normals, and all the public schools of Tennessee which are supported in whole or in part by the public school funds of the state."

A high school biology teacher, John Thomas Scopes (1900-1970) was tried for violating that state law and what might have seemed a trivial matter became a national event. The trial attracted three-time Presidential candidate William Jennings Bryan (1860-1925) to argue for the prosecution and the brilliant Chicago trial lawyer Clarence Darrow (1857-1938) to argue for the defense. America's attention turned toward Dayton as the national press, including the budding radio industry, descended upon this sleepy Tennessee town.

Bryan never gave his closing remarks. Toward the trial's end he suffered a heart attack and died soon after. He had intended to sum up, for both the court and the nation, the trial's true importance. John Scopes' fate was not the issue. He was no more than a pawn in what Bryan called a ". . . battle royal between unbelief that attempts to speak through so-called science and the defenders of the Christian faith, speaking through the legislators of Tennessee.''

The court found Scopes guilty of violating Tennessee law and fined him 100 dollars. Conservatives won in a Tennessee court room, but lost in the court of reason and public opinion. The national media held ''fundamentalism'' up to ridicule as hopelessly ignorant and forever to be relegated to the backwaters of American life.

Yet, nothing could have been further from the truth. Conservatives withdrew, licked their wounds, regrouped and stepped back onto America's national stage stronger than ever. Yet, neither the threats of Rome, the ridicule of Wilberforce, nor the laws of Tennessee could stem science's rising tide.

When conservatives returned to the battle lines in the 1980's, they came armed with a new weapon: creation science. It argues that the scientific evidence actually supports the Bible's view of spontaneous creation, not Darwin's evolutionary theory.

Ironically, conservatives employed science and its methods in a last ditch effort to prop up biblical authority. Ultimately, creation science's argument runs as follows: The Bible is true, reliable, authoritative, and should be accepted on faith. Why? Because science says so. When biblical authority's champions must appeal to science to make their case, science has clearly won the day.

The Liberal Response

Liberals took a different approach, arguing that religion and science were compatible. It is possible to be a modern person and a committed Christian.

Liberals And The Three-Layer World

First, liberals were less threatened by modern science than

conservatives. For them, authority lay with the individual conscience before God, a conscience guided by inspiration, tradition, scripture and community. As a result, they felt little need to defend ancient ideas about the universe that arose 7,000 years ago in the Near East. Liberals saw that many Biblical stories had important symbolic meaning but realized they were not scientific fact.

Take for example the first chapter of Genesis which has caused so much trouble over the past 500 years. What is its meaning for liberals? First, it is by God's will and wisdom that the world exists. Second, for good or ill, we are all in this together — every race, every nation. Third, the basic stuff of life is good. In fact, it is very good indeed.

For liberals, it does not matter if science decides tomorrow that the earth is square and revolves around the moon. It will not change the first chapter of Genesis' meaning.

Two Arenas

Second, liberals contend that science and faith each have their arena. It was a sickly German professor barely five foot tall named Immanuel Kant (1724-1804) who rescued Christianity with one dazzling, decisive stroke. Kant showed that science and faith deal with two different realms. Science's expertise deals with the physical world. Faith, he said, deals with free moral human beings.

The realm of morality, of "what ought to be," belongs to religion not science. As Kant rightly pointed out, science can tell us what is but not what ought to be. It can tell us what a sea gull looks like but not what a sea gull ought to look like. It can tell us what the properties of a circle are but not what they ought to be.

True for circles and sea gulls, it is true for human destiny and morality as well. Consider, for example, Charles Darwin as a young man contemplating his future and asking the eternal human questions, "What should I do with my life? Should I be a doctor, pastor, naturalist? How do I live a good human life in this time and place?" These are exactly the questions science cannot answer.

Now suppose young Charles considers questions of ethics. "Should I kill or not? Should I act with compassion? Should I be honest or dishonest?" Again, science can offer nothing.

True, science has outraced humanity's moral development. It has put into our hands power to destroy the world through nuclear disaster or ecological catastrophe but it has not made us better or wiser men and women.

Science And Meaning

Third, the realm of meaning also belongs to religion. Science works best when it asks the questions "What and How?" but is helpless when confronted with the questions "Why and for What Purpose?"

For example, science now believes it can take us back almost to the very moment of the Big Bang and can adequately explain the universe's evolution from that point until the present.

But suppose we go back a little further, to the time before the great explosion. To the time when everything that now exists was compressed smaller than a human finger tip. Pondering in the dark, silent void, suppose we ask, "Why should anything exist? Why should this bit of matter soon expand to create a vast universe? Why is there anything, rather than nothing?"

Here both faith and science can only stand in silent awe before the mystery of existence.

Evolution

If Darwin's theory hit the conservative church like a

hurricane, for liberals it was more like an overcast summer afternoon. Reactions ranged from cautious to enthusiastic.

By the 20th century, Liberal Christianity had accepted Darwin's basic principle that life evolves. Yet, science was mistaken if it assumed the evolutionary process was purposeless or accidental. Theologians like Kenneth Cauthen insisted God is the source of the evolutionary process that created life on earth and the universe itself. Evolution is not aimless but directed toward the good.

Science maintains that evolution has only the functional aim of creating more efficient plants and animals. It works according to principles that are "random and variable." But is this so?

Liberals contend that every event has an outer appearance and inner meaning. The scientific method can only observe and measure the outer appearance of any process. For example, it can study plants, animals and fossils to see if they change over time. It can do statistical analysis. However, it cannot look inside the process to observe or measure its meaning.

Science has no way to decide if evolution is random or meaningful, pure chance or God's intention. It cannot tell why such a process continues or has taken place at all.

As we have seen, the scientific method lends itself to the study of things that can be observed, measured and expressed in mathematical terms. But as the saying goes, when your only tool is a hammer, everything begins to look like a nail. Using a tool that could not discover the meaning of things and events, science increasingly came to believe the world could not have any meaning to discover.

The Liberal Christian World View

However, we can look at science's facts and come to dramatically different conclusions. Let us begin again with the facts we have gathered and draw conclusions from them, but this time in a different light.

Billions of years ago, all the matter in the visible universe was so dense and compact that it was smaller than a human fingertip. Then a huge explosion occurred: The Big Bang. The divine process of creation had begun. The universe began rapidly expanding, and over billions of years evolved into the multitude of stars, planets and galaxies that exist today.

Further, millions of years ago on earth, a single or a few pools of chemical stew contained all the necessary building blocks for organic life. Perhaps it was a lightning strike that began the seemingly impossible divine plan to bring life from dead matter. Through this process, God created all the living things we now see on earth. Additionally, all was God's intention and ordained from the beginning.

In any case, humans have developed enormous capacities: to think, reason, feel emotion, develop personality and experience personal identity. As hard as it may be to imagine, an extremely intricate chemical process makes all this possible. The "me" that I am is only possible because of unimaginably complex chemical reactions going on within my brain.

Humans are an extraordinary creation. We have evolved from dead matter and like all other organic life forms, we are creatures of earth. In many ways we are the same as monkeys, but we also can write books, paint paintings, build cathedrals. We are spiritual creatures as well, capable of compassion, sacrifice, courage, integrity and self-control. And at this point in history, we are God's co-creators in building the future.

In the West, Christ became the supreme example of humanity because he symbolizes our true identity. We are not merely material creatures like monkeys; nor are we angels, that is, totally spiritual beings. We are both. Like Christ we are both material and spiritual, both of earth and heaven. Capable of reason, compassion and creation, we are truly made in God's image.

Same facts. Different story.

JUNGIAN PSYCHOLOGY AND GOD'S ACTION IN HISTORY

Finally, Christianity can make use of science's powerful tools to serve our vision. In the 3rd century, Origen (182?-254?) said that all the world's learning could be brought home to build the Lord's temple. That was never more true than today.

Jungian psychology has been one field readily accepted by liberal Christians. Many have found that Carl Jung's (1875-1961) psychological views dovetail with liberal thinking and have used them in the fields of spiritual growth, counseling and pastoral care.

Even more important, Jung's psychological approach provides a reasonable way to understand how God works in the world. Christianity has always believed that God works mighty deeds in history, but with modern science's rise, that seemed impossible to maintain. God might work in history, but how was it done?

Jung came to believe God works through the unconscious, a vast and complex web of connections, a web growing layer by layer over thousands of years.

God speaks to every human being to fulfill the divine purposes through the unconscious mind. We realize now that God does not work in history by violating the laws of physics. We know the sun did not really stand still for Joshua and that Moses did not really part the Red Sea. We realize these are symbolic stories.

Instead, God shapes history by working through Moses' unconscious, prompting him to return to Egypt to lead the Israelites out of slavery. Through Saint Paul's dramatic confrontation with the unconscious on the Damascus Road. By sending dreams to the magi warning them not to return to King Herod.

This process has been in motion since human life's beginning on earth and continues through the ages. Sometimes it succeeds as it did with Moses and Saint Paul. Sometimes it fails. Each person is free to act on these promptings or reject them. But always the divine plan moves forward toward its goal.

The divine purpose and the process by which it works, therefore, will always remain a mystery. The unconscious is, by definition, not available to the conscious mind. We cannot know its contents; we only experience its effects. It works slowly and inexorably. We can only guess for what wondrous goals it aims.

SUMMARY

In short, for Liberal Christianity, faith and science are compatible. They are not mortal enemies caught in a death struggle for the modern world's mind and soul. Each has its own arena. For religion: morality and meaning. For science: the physical world and technology. In addition, science can support the Christian vision showing how God works in nature through evolution and in history through the unconscious mind. It is possible to accept science's findings and be a person of faith.

Chapter 4

THE LIFE THAT GOD WOULD GIVE

Holocaust, Hiroshima And The Mystery Of Evil

During the Middle Ages, artisans carved little demons both to decorate the great cathedrals' walls and warn the faithful of hell's torments. But today, that is no longer necessary. During the 20th century, modern humanity has stared directly into the pits of hell. In his book, *The Making of the Atomic Bomb*, Richard Rhodes quotes a young sociologist, one of Hiroshima's survivors.

> *Everything I saw made a deep impression — a park nearby covered with dead bodies waiting to be cremated . . . very badly injured people evacuated in my direction . . . The most impressive thing I saw was some girls, very young girls, not only with their clothes torn off but with their skin peeled off as well . . . My immediate thought was that this was like the hell I had always read about.*

In Chapter 3, we saw how the conflict between science and the three-layer world of the Medieval age raised serious obstacles for modern Christian faith. Yet an even more disturbing problem looms: the mystery of evil and suffering. The 20th century's horrors bring this question home like never before in human history, radically undermining the possibility of belief in a loving God.

Our century has seen two global wars, Stalin's gulags and mass exterminations, Cambodia's killing fields, devastating African famines, napalm and laser guided missiles. And yet we have witnessed two events so monstrous, so terrible, their names have come to symbolize our century's evil and suffering — the Holocaust and Hiroshima.

Granted, humanity must bear responsibility for much of the world's misery. The atomic bomb dropped on Hiroshima was not the work of God. Both the Second World War and the two atomic explosions that brought it to a close were human acts. The extermination of millions by the Nazi regime was a carefully calculated and efficiently organized human plan.

On a smaller scale, human behavior also causes painful suffering. Examples abound.

On the day this paragraph was written, the local newspaper carried the story of a fifteen year old boy at a nearby rural high school. During biology class, he pulled a 9mm pistol from his book bag. Then he fired two shots into the head of a classmate who had tormented and terrorized him for months. That newspaper also told about a woman attacked in a local shopping mall, her throat slashed by a former boyfriend. Pick up a newspaper on any day, in any city, and the story is much the same. Here again, humans must bear the responsibility; God cannot be blamed.

Still, why doesn't God step in? When Nazi gas chambers were operating at peak efficiency, when millions in Africa died agonizing deaths from hunger, when violence stalks modern society, why doesn't God do something?

And what about sickness and disease? What about earthquakes, fire and floods? Why are the innocent allowed to suffer? Even a brief walk through the cancer ward at Philadelphia's Children's Hospital confronts us with this question in stark, heart-rending terms.

Considering the world's immense and unspeakable misery, can modern men and women still believe in a loving God?

The Atheist's Answer

To this question, the atheist answers "No." The hideous agony at Hiroshima and Auschwitz ended forever the notion a loving God exists. The universe is merely a random collection of atoms; suffering and evil are simply part of a universe created by chance.

Therefore, we must make of life what we can. We must summon our courage to struggle against life's absurdity and pain. Even if God does exist, divine actions seem more in keeping with a cruel demon than a loving parent.

The Ant In The Persian Rug

How can Christianity respond to the atheist's challenge? Over the years, both liberal and conservative Christians have offered variations of an answer that might be called "the ant in Persian rug."

Imagine an ant tramping through a magnificent Persian rug's dense wool, searching for crumbs. The ant has no idea the rug possesses an intricate and beautiful design. From the ant's perspective, wandering through the woolen strands, the rug is merely the background of its own struggle for survival. It has no awareness of the rug weaver's glorious master plan.

This viewpoint argues that, like the ant, we cannot see God's magnificent design woven into the universe. Suffering has a part in the divine plan hidden from us by our limited perspective. If we could only see the universe as God sees it, we would realize all things, including suffering, fit together as they should.

God does not create evil, but the divine "permissive will" allows it to exist. Human sin causes much suffering, perhaps most. Although we cannot fully grasp exactly why God allows suffering, it seems, at least in part, because it teaches moral lessons and is necessary for moral development.

In addition, suffering does not have the final word. Eventually, as the New Testament envisions, God will end this world order, punish the wicked and create a new heaven and new earth. In this new world, there will be no more crying, suffering or death. Evil may be real and dreadful but the faithful will be rewarded in the end.

Admittedly, this view has much emotional appeal and many Christians, both liberal and conservative, continue to hold some version of it. Granted, like the universe itself, suffering is a mystery. There are no final, clear cut answers. In addition, we do learn, grow and mature in the cauldron of suffering. Suffering can and often does bring moral development. Further, humans are in no position to decide what a perfect world might be and how much suffering a loving God might permit.

And Yet . . .

And yet, the scale and intensity of the 20th century's misery make this interpretation much harder, if not impossible, to defend. It is far easier to argue for suffering's mystery from a comfortable study or a padded church pew than from Hiroshima's radioactive rubble or a cancer ward's hospital bed. Although this approach does have its own logic and many argue passionately and eloquently for its value and truth, serious problems remain.

Hiroshima's devastation is not the moral equivalent of a spanking or being sent to bed without supper. What moral improvement could be expected from Hiroshima's victims who were vaporized instantly? Who would argue that Hiroshima's bombing was virtuous because young children, with flesh hanging like ragged clothing from their bones, might learn a noble lesson from the experience?

The idea that some day in the future God will set things right does little, if anything, to help. It has been 2,000 years since Saint John's vision of Christ's Second Coming. As the New Testament documents show, the early church measured the time until Jesus' return in weeks, months, a few years. From its earliest days the church has struggled with Jesus' failure to return.

Why the delay? Put aside, for the moment, the problem of Revelation's three-layer world. Simply ask what loving human parents would allow their child to be torn apart by wild beasts in the Roman arena or to waste away at Children's Hospital if they could correct the situation at once? What kind of parents would tell a doctor not to begin life saving treatment just yet because they wanted to teach a moral lesson? If God could have spared the children of Hiroshima and Auschwitz, what possible reason could there be for not doing so?

Granted, no one knows the mind of God, but what kind of God would willingly allow the massive, agonizing suffering that exists? If God can end human suffering with one mighty supernatural act, why not do it and do it now?

A CRUCIFIED GOD

Another possible answer remains. Briefly stated, evil exists because God is all loving but not all powerful. God wills that every creature find fulfillment in the joy of existence and would end suffering immediately, if that were possible. Following the thinking of Kenneth Cauthen, the remainder of the chapter presents this viewpoint. Modern people can squarely face the world's suffering and still believe in the existence of a wise, loving God. Not only is it possible, it is compelling and comforting as well.

Life's Ambiguity

We begin with a simple fact. For all life's suffering, there are moments of pleasure, beauty and joy. For example, walking on the beach listening to the surf's roar, the sea gulls' distinctive screech. Watching the sun rise out of the Atlantic as it turns the sky soft shades of gold, crimson and blue. Or sitting down on a crisp November afternoon for Thanksgiving dinner with family and old friends. Or a springtime stroll through a lilac and azalea filled park, blooming in an irresistible flood of purple, pink and scarlet blossoms.

Thoreau found wonder and goodness at Walden Pond; Emily Dickinson found beauty in her Amherst yard. The French impressionist Claude Monet, in his garden at Giverny. In the midst of the Holocaust, Anne Frank found goodness through a garret window. Harvey Cox, in the secular city's challenge and complexity.

Yet, we know from hard experience that life is a mixture of good and evil, joy and sorrow, pleasure and suffering. Every joyful moment is tinged with sadness; every minute is threatened by suffering, pain and death. The children who bring so much joy must eventually grow up and leave home, perhaps to live in a city a thousand miles away. The friends you have not seen for years must soon leave again. Everyone trembles at the thought of the doctor's solemn diagnosis: cancer. Springtime's blossoms will die; winter will come.

But even atheists do not argue that because of its suffering and uncertainty, life is worthless. Even atheists do not suggest the only rational choice is suicide. In spite of everything, life is worth living.

Why is this so? Why should any good exist? If evil seems to prove that no loving God exists, does good's existence prove the opposite?

We can, for example, combine science's facts with the evil in the world and say, "See, how can there be a loving God when such terrible things sometimes happen?" Yet the reverse is equally plausible. It is possible to look at science's facts and the good in the world and say, "See, there must be a loving God, otherwise, how could such wonderful things ever happen at all?"

In short, the world's pain and suffering does not rule out God's existence, nor does good prove it. In truth, both positions require a leap of faith.

Goodness And Power

Yet if a loving God does exist, how can life's suffering and evil be explained? Traditional Christian teaching holds that God is both all powerful and all good. And this is exactly where the problem lies, in the tension between God's power and goodness.

Considering the world's misery, can we still think of God as both all good and all powerful? If God had the power to gain creation's goal from the very first moment, why did it not happen? If God is all loving and all powerful, why do the innocent suffer? Is God really just an all powerful, cruel demon who could end the anguish of suffering children and starving millions but refuses to do so?

In early 19th century, Friedrich W. Schelling (1775-1854) suggested an alternative to the traditional view. Simply put,

God is all loving, but not all powerful. Something in the very "stuff" of existence hinders God's creating a more perfect world. God struggles to overcome these obstacles that frustrate the divine plan and cause the world's ills. God wants every creature's fulfillment and would quickly end suffering — if only that were possible.

This hardly means God is weak or powerless. Consider creation's wonders. Looking up at the evening sky, that twinkling star on the horizon is just one of a billion fiery suns in an unimaginably awesome universe. Ponder for a moment that its starlight has journeyed trillions of miles to reach the earth. The human eye seeing that light is itself an astonishing creation. Consider the earth's own biosphere that nurtures and sustains life. Clearly these are evidence of divine power beyond human imagination.

The Limits Of Power

Yet, it seems, even God's power has limits. God has given humans freedom but freedom brings with it the possibility of sin. Humans are free to do right or wrong. Sometimes we choose to do the wrong knowing perfectly well that what we are doing is wrong. Apparently, even God cannot create a world that gives freedom to choose but in which evil is never actually chosen.

Equally, we live in a material universe. Like all the earth's creatures, we are flesh and blood. We can and do suffer pain, disease and death. We are born, reach maturity, grow old and die. It appears even God's awesome power cannot create a material world where pain and death play no part.

Finally, as any system increases in size and complexity, it becomes more likely things will go awry. In a system the size of our universe or even with the complexity of the human body, things are bound to go wrong. Even God, it seems, cannot create a fail proof world.

Yet how does this view square with scripture? Actually, the idea of a suffering God fits far better with the Bible's Hebrew vision than the traditional Christian teaching built on Greek philosophical ideas of power and perfection. The Bible opens with the ringing affirmation that God's creation is essentially good, yet almost immediately we find, in fact, existence is corrupted and "fallen." There is a gap between what God wills and what actually exists.

In symbolic language, Adam and Eve's story accounts for the fact of sin and death. Within the garden's womb, humanity lives in endless bliss. Yet once thrown into real life, in the land east of Eden, humans must make hard moral choices and endure work, pain and death.

In addition, the Bible assumes other cosmic powers exist along with God. These demonic forces oppose and frustrate the divine will, and in turn, God must struggle against and overcome them.

In the New Testament, the gospels assert that God seeks to save humanity, bringing all into a kingdom of fulfillment and love. Christ's cross reveals God's true nature: not as one who remains aloof, unmoved and untouched in heaven, but who enters the world to battle on the side of love and justice. Yet in this clash, Jesus is not pictured as a great military genius, but as a wounded savior. Here, God suffers with creation and its creatures, bearing the wounds of evil on the cross.

A Helpful Metaphor

Nicholas Berdyaev provides a helpful metaphor of God's relationship to the world. Early in his life, Berdyaev believed in communism and later converted to philosophy. During World War II, in a Nazi death camp he had his final conversion.

One morning, the prisoners lined up as the commandant counted out those to die that day. The lot fell to a woman and her young child. The mother pleaded that her child be spared but the commandant would not yield.

Also in line was a woman known to the other prisoners only as Mother Maria. Realizing the Nazi officer was only interested in the right numbers, Mother Maria pushed forward and took the child's place. She would die that day, the child would live.

Berdyaev understood for the first time the love of which Christians speak. This woman had put on Christ's role, willingly took upon herself another's suffering. This was God's suffering love.

The gospels do not portray God's redeeming power sweeping away evil with a dramatic bang but as a lamb led to slaughter. God's power may have limits, but God's love does not.

The Triumph Of God

Does this mean there are no victories for good? Does evil always win?

In his poem, "The Present Crisis," James Russell Lowell wrote, "Truth forever on the scaffold, Wrong forever on the throne, — Yet that scaffold sways the future . . ." Just as the cross reveals God's suffering love, the resurrection lays bare the future's meaning. God suffers and struggles with suffering, struggling humanity. God does not work in history by violating the laws of physics. Instead the divine will works through an evolutionary process and guides history through the human unconscious to advance its purposes. There are defeats and reversals, but there are real victories as well.

For example, Lowell's poem first appeared in the Boston *Courier* on December 11, 1844, to oppose the annexation of Texas into the American union as a slave state. Over the next decade, the issue of slavery and freedom continued to bubble until it finally exploded in civil war.

The years from 1861 until 1865 saw suffering unlike anything before on the American continent. The battle of Bull Run, Chancellorsville, Gettysburg, the burning of Atlanta brought untold suffering and grief to millions. Yet from that misery came a victory for good and slavery's end. The success was real and the world's life moved forward. The cross of Christ does sway the future.

Admittedly, the Civil War did not solve all America's problems of freedom, race and human dignity as our century has shown. Yet all victories in this world are partial and provisional. New ones must continually be won. Granted, divine progress is slow; divine justice is inexact. Still, the victories are real. God suffers and struggles with us, continually seeking to move all creation toward divine goals.

THE WORLD TO COME

Since prehistoric times, human beings have hoped for life beyond death. Food, weapons and utensils buried in ancient tombs bear silent witness to the hope of paradise. Judaism, Christianity, Islam and many other religions have found comfort in the promise that death is only a door to a new and transformed life.

Does another spiritual realm exist? Does heaven wait beyond the grave? Many modern people casually reject such a possibility as hopelessly naive, yet who can say for sure? Recent scientific advances have made belief in a spiritual world more reasonable, not less. Near death experiences, dreams, neuroscience and the very improbability of the universe itself, all leave the door ajar. Although, clearly, there are no certain answers, fascinating possibilities remain.

Near Death Experiences

First, many today argue "near death" experiences are evidence for life beyond this world. In recent years, medical technology's advance made it possible to revive patients who were clinically dead. Then something totally unexpected began to happen.

After recovering, these patients began to tell incredible stories about leaving their bodies, of hovering above the operating table, watching and listening, as the doctors worked to save them. Even more astounding were stories of traveling down a tunnel, of being greeted by a being of light. Not surprisingly, these people returned to their lives with new inner peace and confidence in human immortality. Although "near death" experiences are not hard, conclusive proof of another world, they are intriguing.

The Realm Of Dreams

Second, dreams provide a fascinating hint of what might be. Each night we descend into a mysterious world, a world much like death. But where do dreams come from? Do they come from another, spiritual realm? Are they merely chemical reactions in the brain? In fact, no one knows. They are as mysterious as the universe itself.

Neuroscience And The Soul

Third, in an interview about brain function with Bill Moyer, neuroscientist Dr. Candice Pert tells about an energy that seems to leave the body at death.

> *. . . I feel that the person who will figure this out is going to be a physicist, because clearly there's another form of energy that we have not yet understood. For example,*

> *there's a form of energy that appears to leave the body when it dies. If we call that another energy that just hasn't been discovered yet, it sounds much less frightening to me than "spirit." Remember, I'm a scientist, and in the Western tradition I don't use the word "spirit." "Soul" is a four letter word in our tradition.*

The Mystery Of The Universe

Fourth, scientists tell us everything in the visible universe was once the size of a human finger tip, perhaps smaller than an atom. Yet today the nearest star is a mind boggling 25,500,000,000,000 miles from earth. In addition, the physicist Sir Arthur Eddington (1882-1944) asked a puzzling question that raises doubts about the very way we understand ordinary reality. Is that desk you write on really solid, hard and substantial? Or, is it mostly empty space and whirling atoms? Or, is it both?

What is real and what is illusion? What is possible and what is not? In a universe like ours, who can say what the real "facts" might be. Granted, we have no evidence consciousness can exist without a physical body, but we have no evidence it cannot.

As Ken Cauthen notes, if you looked at the universe a few million years after the "Big Bang," you might easily decide nothing special was happening. Yet how wrong you would have been. A universe where time is measured in billions of years and distance by light years calls for a certain amount of humility. Who knows what a loving God might have in mind? Who knows what glories might still be to come, in this world or in another?

The Nicene Creed takes a helpful approach. It states, ". . . and we look for the resurrection of the dead, and the life of the world to come." Here, hope, not evidence, is finally the key. The future's comfort comes from confidence that our destiny is in God's hands. We look forward with hope and hope has no limits.

RESPONDING TO SUFFERING

This chapter offered possible answers to evil's mystery for consideration but one thing is certain. There will be suffering. Yet, we can choose how we respond to life's harsh realities. We can let them make us cynical and bitter or strive to live with as much joy as circumstances permit.

Living With Joy

A remarkable and helpful story comes from Central America. During the 1980's turmoil, a news report came from a small village where rampaging government and rebel armies had come repeatedly, killing, raping and stealing. At last, the chaos drove these villagers across the border to live as refugees. Yet they soon found life in a refugee camp worse than living in a war zone and finally returned home.

How did they survive and, in fact, live with joy? A village leader explained that every day the war did not bring terror and death, every minute lived in peace, was seen as a moment to savor and celebrate. All of us might learn a lesson here.

The Cauldron Of Suffering

Second, suffering does challenge us to grow, forcing us to examine our behavior, values and potential. Although it does not always do so, it can make us more sensitive to other's pain and push us to new levels of maturity and achievement.

During the 20th century, perhaps no one provides a more dramatic example than Helen Keller (1880-1968). Although blind and deaf from the age of 19 months, she graduated with honors from Radcliffe College in 1904 and became a celebrated writer, lecturer and scholar. She wrote of her struggles, "I learned that it is possible for us to create light, sound, and order no matter what calamity may befall us in the outer world."

Commitment To Compassion

Third, we can work to ease what suffering we can. For example, a few years ago a morning news program carried the story of a woman in Boston. During the autumn, she discovered an injured robin in her yard. All the rest had long since flown south for the winter.

She took the robin into her home and nursed it back to health. When it was ready to be released, she had it flown by air express to Miami and arranged for an animal shelter to meet the flight to free this tiny creature for its new life.

When asked why she had gone to so much trouble and expense for one bird, she explained that, as a Holocaust survivor, she had lived through a time when there was no compassion or concern for life. She promised herself that, if she survived, she would honor every creature, no matter how small.

"Look at the birds of the air;" Jesus said, "they neither sow nor reap nor gather into barns, and yet your heavenly Father feeds them. Are you not of more value than they?" (Matthew 6:26 NRSV). Indeed.

SUMMARY

In this chapter we have seen that evil's mystery does not rule out belief in a loving God's existence. Christianity trusts a God who suffers with creation, who's love is infinite even if divine power is not. Just as Christ's cross symbolizes God's suffering love, the resurrection symbolizes the future's hope. God continually seeks to move creation and its creatures toward life fulfilling joy. All can join the struggle to bear the world's burdens and ease its pain.

The Medieval Christian vision, symbolized by Saint-Denis, had been decaying for 500 years before it was finally shattered at Hiroshima. But now, looking over the rubble, the situation no longer seems so hopeless.

Perhaps the ring of hammer against chisel and stone can be heard again. Perhaps the shattered glass can be made even more magnificent than before. In the next chapter we start rebuilding Christianity's foundations. We look at how modern biblical research has changed the Medieval view of scripture. We examine the liberal method for interpreting the Bible and how it can unlock scripture's power for the modern world.

Chapter 5

UPON THE SOLID ROCK

Conflict And Controversy

For the past 200 years, the Bible has been surrounded by confusion and controversy. Is it God's literal word without error or contradiction as conservative Protestants claim? Was the Bible dictated to scribes who merely passed on what they were told to write? Yet if this is true, how can you account for the teaching that the world does not move? That the sun stood still for Joshua, and other passages modern people know cannot be literally true?

On the other hand, atheists and skeptics argue the Bible is no more than just another ancient book. It may teach a few praiseworthy moral principles but for the most part contains nothing but outdated legends and outright lies about a nonexistent God. Atheists argue that the Bible only fosters ignorance, superstition and bigotry. Even worse, it salves middle class conscience and serves to keep the poor content with promises of "pie in the sky" while the privileged reap life's benefits.

Liberal Christianity takes a different view. The Bible is not just any book, as atheists think; nor is it God's literal words as conservatives claim. Liberals contend the Bible reveals a loving God who has created the world and works to bring it to fulfillment. It contains a variety of literature and stories written with the ideas, images and mythic language of a prescientific age. Some must be interpreted symbolically. Some have greater value than others.

SYMBOLIC INTERPRETATION

The conflict between faith and knowledge has become critical during the 20th century. The Bible contains powerful and invaluable stories, but when taken literally, they come into impossible conflict with science. Here, guided by Carl Jung's thinking, we see that if the church continues to demand belief in what moderns know is not true, it risks a massive and disastrous rejection of Christianity.

When modern men and women force themselves to believe what they know cannot be, secret doubts arise that must be quickly repressed. The stronger the doubts, the more powerful the repression must be. It is well known in psychology that this process often ends in fanaticism.

In the 1980's, for example, a conservative Protestant denomination fired a seminary professor. Although he accepted the doctrine of Christ's literal virgin birth, he was dismissed for being willing to allow others to hold a different position. Similarly, an American Roman Catholic Cardinal visited his local seminary and announced to staff and students that in the future there would be no dissent. These actions are completely understandable. To keep doubts repressed, all opposition must be stamped out and all dissent stifled.

But it may be that one morning 50 or 50,000 or 50,000,000 Christians will wake up and say, "I just cannot believe this.

I do not believe this and I cannot make myself believe this anymore."

What would such a rejection mean? What would happen to the West and the world's future if there were a complete repudiation of Christianity and its values? What if Western society's spiritual and moral foundation, as fragile as it already may be, would totally collapse? Who can imagine the far-reaching consequences of such a calamity?

The risks are great but, as Jung argues, a showdown between faith and science is unnecessary. The Bible and the creeds can be interpreted symbolically. Christianity need not defend a 7,000-year-old prescientific world view.

Christian faith trusts a loving, living God, not the idea that Jesus was born of a virgin or that a great fish swallowed Jonah. Interpreting the Bible symbolically resolves the conflict between science and faith. Christianity loses nothing and the danger of a sudden spiritual collapse fades.

Nor is this idea new. During the 3rd century, 1,200 years before Copernicus, the church father Origen realized some biblical stories could not be taken literally. Looking at the Genesis creation account, he understood the world could not possibly have been made in six literal 24-hour days. Why? Because the sun was not created until the fourth day! How, he asked, could there be morning and evening before the sun was made? Origen reasoned the author clearly must have had some symbolic meaning in mind.

Understanding The Bible's Supernatural Stories

What then can we make of the Bible's supernatural stories? In the 18th century a German professor named Johann Semler (1725-1791) saw the answer. He pointed out that the Bible reveals God's will but its authors thought and wrote within the context of their time.

Obviously, the biblical writers lived in a prescientific age. Their understanding of the world, its creation and development came from stories common among the ancient Near East's peoples. Like their neighbors, they believed that God spoke in thunder; punished the wicked with sickness, drought and flood; rewarded the virtuous with riches, health and bountiful harvests. The idea of virgin births and demonic possessions did not puzzle them. They knew nothing about Copernicus, Newton, Darwin, Freud or Einstein. Therefore, they simply told their story using the ideas and images of their day.

During Jesus' time, for example, many people were thought to perform "signs and wonders." Yet these were not miracles as modern people understand the term: that is, a violation of known scientific law. The ancients knew of no scientific law to violate. In fact, they took for granted that God regularly took part in human affairs and the working of nature. That Jesus does wonders amazes no one in the gospels. His followers and the crowds are only astonished by his wonder's magnitude and his enemies only question if his power comes from God or Satan.

But, as modern science advanced in the 18th and 19th centuries, it became clear the Bible's supernatural stories could no longer be taken literally. Many liberal scholars thought that the only possible solution was simply to reject them.

For example, Heinrich Paulus (1761-1851) did just that suggesting the gospel's supernatural occurrences were really natural events that the disciples simply misunderstood. Jesus did not really walk on water; his disciples only thought he did as they saw him walking along the shore through the mist. The feeding of the 5,000 was not really miraculous; Jesus' own generosity in sharing the little he had merely inspired the crowd to do the same.

In his classic work *The Life of Jesus*, David Friedrich Strauss (1808-1874) realized Paulus' rational explanations were clearly ridiculous. Yet he agreed the gospel's supernatural events could not be historical facts and insisted Christ's life must be examined as any other important historical figure. Still, Strauss could not ignore the gospels are full of miracles. He finally concluded they must have been natural events in Jesus' life that were covered over by myths.

The subject came up again in the 20th century when the German scholar Rudolf Bultmann called for "demythologizing" the Bible. Bultmann believed the Bible's mythic stories must be translated into non-mythic language to make them understandable to modern men and women.

Myth And The Bible's Interpretation

In contrast, Jung argued liberal scholarship was on the wrong track. First, it did not go far enough, and second, it did not understand myth's religious importance. Simply, the Bible's mythic stories could not be discarded without doing Christianity irreparable harm.

From his study of psychology, Jung understood that myth is religion's lifeblood. Mythic stories like those of gods and goddesses, angels and demons, the world's creation and destruction, are psychological facts and symbolically true. They have a real existence within the unconscious mind and powerfully express themselves through it. In addition, they cannot be eliminated or destroyed. They can be dismissed or suppressed but only to reappear in distorted and often sinister forms. We cannot deny them for long and we ignore them only at our peril.

For example, consider what happened when communism came to power in the Soviet Union. The government officially repressed religious faith, banned the Bible, converted churches into museums and closed seminaries. Yet, religious impulses did not disappear. They merely changed shape, taking the form of a stern and rigidly dogmatic faith in communism.

The Soviet state wielded godlike power with many rules and little mercy. The religious idea of "fear of God" was more than adequately replaced by fear of the secret police. Those who questioned orthodox State policy were considered secular heretics and banished to Siberia or psychiatric hospitals. Communism had its own creed that called for devotion and sacrifice to gain an inevitable victory. It promised a future paradise, not in heaven, but on earth. Finally, like saints' relics in a medieval cathedral, Lenin and Stalin were preserved in a secular shrine for the faithful to visit.

In short, the religious impulses even of devout atheists did not vanish. They were merely transformed into a devilish parody of Christian faith.

Without doubt, religious impulses do exist and express themselves through the unconscious mind. The Christian myths are not just fairy tales that modern men and women can reject and cast aside. They are psychological facts that have a real and powerful existence within us. They cannot be thrown out nor exchanged for rational explanations.

The great stories of Moses' parting of the Red Sea, Daniel in the lion's den and Christ's virgin birth are essential. They must be treasured, told and retold, as they have been for 2,000 years, but they must be interpreted symbolically.

An Example: Jonah And The Great Fish

Let us turn now to an example: the story of Jonah and the great fish. Obviously impossible from a scientific viewpoint, but what symbolic meaning might it hold? Briefly, we have the story of a man who runs from God and his destiny. Boarding a ship to escape, a storm wreaks havoc on his conscious plans. Thrown overboard, a great fish swallows Jonah, symbolizing the descent into the unconscious. Fish, water and ocean are all mythic symbols that reappear throughout the world's religious literature. After three days, Jonah returns to the world of consciousness as a transformed person. His experience within the depths moves him to a new level of existence.

A literal interpretation of Jonah might focus on God's power over nature: namely, that God created a storm to prevent Jonah's escape and ordered a fish to deliver him back to land. A symbolic interpretation does not deny God's power but sees these stories as metaphors. In addition, such an approach expands the story's spiritual depth and it does not conflict with scientific knowledge.

Can The Text Mean Anything We Want?

Some may object that symbolic interpretation makes it possible to read anything into the text and, of course, that danger does exist. Yet no method of interpreting the Bible is totally objective. Scholars, preachers and Bible students throughout history have often found what they wanted in the Bible's texts and have done so honestly believing themselves to be objective. Yet no matter how hard we try, the author's assumptions, life situation and unconscious processes shape every method.

The Quaker movement learned as much during the 17th century. John Naylor, a leader among London Quakers, decided to imitate Christ's triumphal entry by riding a donkey into Bristol, England, accompanied by loud hosannas. But Bristol was not Jerusalem and Naylor was not Christ. Although pleading his intention had only been to symbolize Christ's coming into human hearts, Quakers were horrified. Local authorities were even less sympathetic and ordered the letter 'B' burned into his forehead for blasphemy, bored a hole through his tongue and threw him in prison.

The Quakers did eventually learn to temper symbolic interpretation and individual freedom with tradition's guidance and the community's friendly persuasion. Liberals can do the same.

The Bible's symbolic interpretation does present problems. Yet what is our purpose in studying the Bible? Is it merely to find "the right answers" to justify our own most cherished ideas and opinions? Or, do we read the Bible to seek the living God? To allow the divine will to shape our beliefs and us? Clearly, as Jonah discovered, when God moves in human lives all our conscious plans and favorite opinions may be remolded by God's will.

Does The Bible Have Historical Value?

Though we have seen the Bible's mythic, supernatural stories cannot be taken literally, the Bible does contain much that is historically accurate as archeological research has proved. During the second half of the 20th century we have learned a great deal about the ancient world's daily life, its great historical movements and especially about ancient manuscripts. Perhaps no find has been more impressive than the discovery in 1992 of the tomb of Caiaphas whom the gospels identify as the high priest who presided at Jesus' trial before the Sanhedrin.

Yet no archeological research can prove or disprove a loving God's existence. In John's gospel, the disciple Thomas is skeptical when he first hears of Christ's resurrection. He says, ". . . Unless I see the mark of the nails in his hands, and put my finger in the mark of the nails and my hand in his side, I will not believe" (John 20:25b NRSV). Notice, Thomas does not say, "Unless someone discovers Caiaphas' tomb . . ."

The point is this. No archeological discovery of any kind can prove the Bible's truth no matter how interesting or important it may be.

THE SOLID ROCK

Cross And Resurrection

Along with his insight that the biblical writers thought and wrote within the context of their time, Johann Semler made a second key observation. Not all scripture is of equal value.

Every Christian viewpoint whether liberal, fundamentalist, neo-orthodox, or whatever, sees some scriptural passages as more important than others. For example, Martin Luther believed Paul's letter to the Romans held the key to scripture and salvation:

> *For I am not ashamed of the gospel; it is the power of God for salvation to everyone who has faith, to the Jew first and also to the Greek. For in it the righteousness of God is revealed through faith for faith; as it is written, "The one who is righteous will live by faith" (Romans 1:16-17 NRSV).*

Luther's meditation on this passage led to his doctrine of "justification by faith alone."

But, Luther found other Bible passages that were not to his liking. For example, he loathed James' letter that states, "So faith by itself, if it has no works, is dead" (James 2:17 NRSV). Here, the text's plain meaning seems to support the view that salvation requires both faith and good works. It was a viewpoint Luther despised and he denounced James' letter as the "epistle of straw."

In short, Luther did not give equal weight to all scripture, nor did Calvin, nor does anyone else. Every Christian viewpoint sees some texts as more valuable than others.

What about Liberal Christianity? What biblical texts provide the foundation for liberal belief? The answer is clear: Christ's cross and resurrection. Tradition, scholarship and spiritual insight mark these passages as most important. They show more clearly than anywhere else in the Bible the height, breadth and depth of God's compassion. For Liberal Christianity, faith's solid rock is God's infinite suffering love symbolically revealed on the cross. It is this yardstick of compassion, humility, mercy and forgiveness by which all biblical texts, beliefs and moral actions must be judged.

The Cross' Meaning

Why, then, was it necessary for Jesus to go to the cross? Over the centuries, three basic answers have been offered.

The Ransom Theory

Origen gave the first important explanation stating that the sin committed in the Garden of Eden made humanity captive to the devil. God wanted to bring salvation, but could not do so because the devil had a just claim to human souls. The only solution was for God to ransom captive humanity like a kidnap victim. To provide the devil with a sufficiently valuable prize, God could only offer Jesus in humanity's place.

The Debt Theory

Anselm (1033-1109) presented a second viewpoint. He argued that sin creates a debt to God that humans are completely unable to repay. Only a perfect, sinless human could make good the debt owed to the offended divine justice and majesty. Therefore, Christ's death on the cross paid the obligation but because Christ was perfect, some merit was left over. It is through this "left over" merit that Christ earns humanity's salvation.

In the 20th century, these explanations create more problems than they solve. Why must God kill Jesus to repay a debt? How can Jesus' death pay a ransom to the devil? How could such a death actually change the human situation?

The difficulty comes from the dramatically different ways modern and ancient people understand the world. Both Origen's and Anselm's explanations depend on a three-layer universe with all its supernatural beings and events. In this view, Jesus' saving work is a cosmic drama played out on a three-layer world stage. Jesus comes down to earth from a heaven "up there," is born of a virgin, works wonders, dies, is resurrected and ascends again to heaven. At some time in the future he will return with his angels to bring a fiery end to this three-layer world and create a new heaven and new earth.

But what if there is no heaven "up there" from which Jesus can descend and to which he can return? What if there are no stars hung from the firmament that can fall at the last trumpet's sound? What does this mean for Jesus' saving work upon the cross if no such three-layer world exists?

The Awakening Of Compassion

The brilliant, controversial scholar Peter Abelard (1079-1142) gave the most promising answer for moderns. Abelard taught that Jesus went to the cross, not as a ransom, nor to repay a debt, but to awaken compassion in the human heart. To see Christ's death on the cross is to see God's loving attitude toward humanity from the beginning. To witness Christ's suffering is to see the suffering of all life and awaken human hearts to a spiritual second birth.

A second, spiritual birth is an important religious idea not limited to Christianity. True, some conservative churches did use the slogan "born again Christian" as a rallying cry during the late 20th century. But, a spiritual rebirth has a more important and profound meaning than accepting a catalog of conservative religious beliefs and a right wing political agenda.

In Christian tradition, the key words appear in John's gospel when Jesus tells the Jewish teacher Nicodemus:

> *. . . Very truly, I tell you, no one can enter the kingdom of God without being born from above. Nicodemus said to him, 'How can anyone be born after having grown old? Can one enter a second time into the mother's womb and be born?' Jesus answered, 'Very truly, I tell you, no one can enter the Kingdom of God without being born of water and the Spirit. What is born of the flesh is flesh, and what is born of the Spirit is spirit' (John 3:3-6 NRSV).*

That which is born of flesh is flesh. Humans are born with a whole-hearted devotion to this world's things and its pleasures. Each of us is a born materialist. Our central concerns are two: self preservation and preservation of the species, that is, survival and sex.

But that which is born of Spirit is spirit. Throughout the world's religions, the need for a second birth is clear. As we grow older, our appetites and ambitions may become more mature, more sophisticated, but without a spiritual rebirth we remain at the animal, material level.

Abelard saw that to ponder Christ's suffering death on the cross could open the door to a spiritual awakening. It can move us from too much devotion to this world and toward devotion to the spiritual realm.

Historical Events?

As we have seen, Liberal Christianity believes the cross and resurrection are the most profound expressions of God's suffering love for the world. But again, we must be clear. Christian faith is in God's love revealed symbolically in the biblical texts. We trust God's love, not stories in a book, not even if that book is the Bible.

But are the cross and resurrection historical facts like Abraham Lincoln's assassination or the Battle of Waterloo?

There is no reason to doubt the crucifixion is an historical event. Granted, Jewish and Roman historians give almost no information about Jesus and precious little about the earliest church. Yet taken together, the biblical accounts, the early church fathers' writings and the church's subsequent development makes no other view believable. The great mainstream of Roman and Jewish life may have had little interest in an obscure Galilean preacher's death or his first followers. Yet there is no reason to doubt that Jerusalem's Roman government executed Jesus of Nazareth on charges of sedition in about 33 A.D.

But by itself, the cross is just another visionary moral teacher's death at the hands of powerful, calculating enemies. A tragedy not unlike a million other deaths from Socrates to Martin Luther King. Add the resurrection, however, and the cross moves from history's field of time and space to the eternal. It becomes as Paul said, "The wisdom of God."

The historical problem, therefore, is not the cross but the resurrection. This is a far more difficult question. First, the idea is hard, perhaps impossible for moderns to accept. Second, the resurrection stories themselves include two complex traditions: the record of Jesus's appearances and the empty tomb.

Liberals are, in fact, divided about the resurrection. Some accept it as symbolic story, others as literal historical fact. Ancient Judaism was also divided about belief in a general resurrection of the dead. Among Jewish groups the Pharisees accepted the idea, the Sadducees rejected it. Therefore, when Paul's first audience read, "But in fact Christ has been raised from the dead, the first fruits of those who have died" (1 Corinthians 15:20 NRSV), they would have understood it quite differently than we do today.

Sadducees would have rejected Paul's statement as impossible. Pharisees, however, would have realized Paul was claiming the general resurrection had begun and that Jesus was just the first of many to be raised. The idea of the resurrection would not have shocked them. Only the timing would have been in question.

For modern men and women, the situation is radically different. Moderns ask, "Is it possible for a corpse dead three days in the tomb to come back to life, even if that corpse is Jesus?"

Jesus' Resurrection Appearances

Despite modern doubts, there can be no question that Jesus' eleven remaining disciples along with many other followers became convinced Jesus was alive and had risen from the dead. Clearly, some experience changed a scattered, frightened band into a determined, fearless, militant church: a church that challenged and defeated the Roman Empire in spite of persecution, torture and death. Yet, what was this experience and what can we uncover about it 2,000 years later?

First, we know that Paul's letters provide the earliest resurrection accounts, namely, Jesus' appearances to his followers. In his letter to the Corinthians he says:

> *For I handed on to you as of first importance what I in turn had received: that Christ died for our sins in accordance with the scriptures, and that he was buried, and that he was raised on the third day in accordance with the scriptures, and that he appeared to Cephas, then to the twelve. Then he appeared to more than five hundred brothers and sisters at one time, most of whom are still alive, though some have died. Then he appeared to James, then to all the apostles. Last of all, as to one untimely born, he appeared also to me (1 Corinthians 15:3-8 NRSV).*

Second, those who insisted they had seen the risen Christ changed dramatically. Paul, who was the church's most determined persecutor, became its most zealous missionary, creative thinker and powerful writer. At first, Paul terrified the early church. When he finally traveled to meet the elders in Jerusalem, his arrival sent shivers through the church's leadership. They could hardly accept that the one who had hunted them down, who had stood by approvingly when their brother Stephen was stoned to death, was now a believer.

The Dying Rising God

What can account for the resurrection experiences and these dramatic changes in Paul and others? The study of comparative mythology provides insight into what may have happened and how it occurred.

We know the idea of a dying rising god is not unique to Christianity. Religions across the world have believed in a god who dies and returns to life bringing back benefits for humanity.

Joseph Campbell points to a traditional story told by the Algonquin peoples about a dying and rising corn god. A handsome young prince appears wearing a green plume and orders that he be killed, cut up, buried and his grave be carefully tended. Soon a vigorous patch of corn is growing over the prince's grave. Thus, the prince, actually the corn god, is reborn in the year's harvest providing food for his earthly children.

As Campbell made clear, almost identical stories come from all over the world. Although the plant may change, the story remains the same. The dying rising god brings food just as death transforms Christ's body into the spiritual food of bread and wine for the Lord's Supper.

The mythic story of Osiris, the Egyptian god of death and rebirth, was almost certainly known among those living in nearby Palestine. Apparently, opponents accused the church of simply patterning its teaching about Jesus on the Osiris myth or another like it.

The Second Letter of Peter denies these charges saying, "For we did not follow cleverly devised myths when we made known to you about the power and coming of our Lord Jesus Christ, but we had been eyewitnesses of his majesty" (2 Peter 1:16 NRSV). In short, the church argued that what had been just a mythic story had now become an historical fact in Jesus Christ.

Jungian psychology has shown themes like the dying rising savior are basic building blocks within the human psyche. These themes, or archetypes as Jung calls them, express themselves through our unconscious mind. They have an independent life within us and produce very powerful effects.

Considering what we know about the unconscious and the dying rising savior archetype, it is reasonable to conclude that Christ appeared to his followers as a powerful inner experience. His resurrection appearances were psychological facts whether they were outwardly visible or not.

Second Peter rightly states the early church did not intentionally use the dying rising savior theme to create their teaching about Jesus. It may be these archetypal stories used them. God working through the human unconscious shaped the church's developing message. Here, the story of the dying rising god came to its fullest, most sophisticated and ultimate expression in Christ. And in this way, revealed God's will to the world.

The Empty Tomb's Discovery

As difficult as the appearance reports may be, the gospel's empty tomb stories are even more problematic. First, although scholars argue endlessly about when the gospels were written, it seems likely to have been sometime between 60 and 110 A.D. There is general agreement that Mark's gospel was written first and John's, last. In any case, the gospels were written some years after the event. Second, Paul does not seem to know about this tradition. Third, the writers give markedly different accounts.

It is significant that Paul, the earliest of the resurrection accounts, does not mention an empty tomb. Although he tells about Jesus' appearances, he either did not know about the empty tomb tradition, did not think it decisive, or chose for another reason not to include it in his letters that now appear in the New Testament.

In the gospel accounts, Mark tells us three women, Mary Magdalene, Mary the mother of James, and Salome, went to the tomb. They discover it empty except for a young man dressed in a white robe who tells them Jesus has risen from the dead. Yet, Luke says it was Mary Magdalene, Mary, Joanna and "others" who went. They meet two men wearing clothes that gleam like lightning. Matthew tells us it was two women who see an angel roll the stone from the tomb's entrance. John says Mary went alone.

In John's gospel, Peter and "the disciple whom Jesus loved" rush to the tomb to see for themselves; in Luke only Peter goes. Matthew does not mention anyone going back to the tomb. Mark is even more obscure. Some scholars believe the original ending of Mark has been lost. But, if Mark is complete as we now have it, the terrified women tell no one what they have found. Therefore, the disciples never find out the tomb is empty at all!

Jesus' Resurrection Body

The gospel stories also conflict over the nature of Jesus' resurrection body, sometimes picturing Jesus like a ghost, sometimes like a flesh and blood human being.

In Luke, Jesus vanishes before the eyes of his two followers on the Emmaus road. Yet later, he tells the disciples to touch him and see that he is not a ghost but flesh and bones. In John, he tells Mary Magdalene not to hold him because he has not yet ascended to the Father. Shortly after, he suddenly appears in a locked room where the disciples are in hiding. Yet, he then tells Thomas to touch the marks of the nails and the spear.

Historic Fact Or Symbolic Story?

What then can be said about the cross and resurrection? Are they historic fact or symbolic story? No one can seriously deny the cross is an historical event. Jesus of Nazareth was crucified by the orders of Judea's Roman government and soon after his followers began to insist he had risen from the dead and had appeared to them. Often they were willing to die for this conviction.

In what way Jesus appeared to his followers is far less clear. That it was an inner, psychological event seems most likely but this can never be known for sure.

What about the empty tomb? Consider the following. First, the four gospels were most likely written between 30 to 80 years after the crucifixion giving us conflicting accounts. Second, Paul seems unaware of the tradition. Third, 1st century Jewish thinking could not imagine existence without a body of flesh and bone. Therefore, it seems reasonable to conclude the gospel writers used the empty tomb as a metaphor to express the resurrection's spiritual truth.

From the beginning, mystery has shrouded the resurrection but this much is clear. Liberal Christianity can welcome both those who hold the resurrection to be historical fact and those who hold it to be symbolic story. Both are possible Christian positions.

Despite the way we view the Bible's cross and resurrection accounts, their meaning is plain. Both point to human renewal and the transformation of the universe itself. Together, they show God's true nature. Jesus' death is not just any death, but *the death* that reveals God's infinite love for the world.

SUMMARY

When the Medieval world's great cathedrals were built, massive foundations supported the church's enormous weight. Workers lavished as much care on these gigantic stones deep beneath the surface as on the towers that would be seen for miles.

But over the past 500 years, Medieval Christianity's structure was shaken, first by the Renaissance and Reformation, and then by the onslaught of scientific, political, industrial and technological revolution. Built on a foundation of rigid authority, the Medieval vision collapsed under the strain. It continues now within conservative churches, as Shakespeare said, "a walking shadow." Although often full of sound and fury, it signifies nothing more than a completely understandable but desperate attempt to fight off despair in a chaotic modern world.

In contrast, for the past 200 years, liberals have worked to reestablish Christianity's foundations. Liberals maintain that modern men and women need not reject the scientific and cultural advances of the last 500 years to be committed Christians. The Bible does reveal God, but its mythic, supernatural stories must be interpreted symbolically.

In addition, not all scripture is of equal value. Liberal Christianity does not build on a foundation of blind obedience to church authority nor upon the Bible as God's literal words. Instead, it rises upon the solid rock of God's love, a love revealed symbolically in Christ's cross and resurrection. A love that calls everyone to renewal and the world to transformation in Christ's image.

Chapter 6

OUR NOBLEST CREEDS

More Than Experience

In the last chapter, we saw that faith begins with experience; something happens that inspires trust in God. And yet we humans want more than experience. We want to understand our experience and our world. We want to share our understanding with others.

Through the ages, Christians have tried to express their experience in the historic creeds and the great theologies. From the beginning, creeds and beliefs have served important functions. They have helped us understand Christianity's meaning and implications, created social unity within the church and explained Christianity to the world.

Therefore, here we summarize liberal belief. We lay out its design principles, its four pillars and the mortar and stone with which it builds.

But before we move on, a few words of caution are needed. First, beliefs are not the same as religious experience. They may help us draw near experience but are not a substitute for it. Second, no matter how profound their meaning, beliefs can never fully express the relationship between God and the believer. To paraphrase James Ashbrook, we always experience more than we know; we always know more than we can say. Finally, as history has so often shown, beliefs can become a powerful weapon to enforce conformity and compliance rather than to draw people closer to an experience of God.

Our dilemma is plain. How can the inexpressible be expressed? Admittedly, the task is perilous; indeed, impossible. And yet we must still attempt to speak about God and the divine will.

DESIGN PRINCIPLES

When Europe's great cathedrals were built, a basic design principle played on the tension between height and length. Entering Chartres cathedral, your gaze is pulled up toward the peak of its lofty 121-foot vault. Then forward, along the nave's 130-foot length. Everything directs attention toward the altar where God and humanity meet.

In other cathedrals the same principle held true. Not to be outdone by Chartres, the vault at Reims cathedral rose to 125 feet. Then Amiens climbed to 139 feet. Rising to an astonishing 158 feet, Beauvais cathedral soared above them all. Higher and longer was the goal to create the breathtaking view the Medieval world loved so much.

Modern And Christian

Liberal Christianity has its own design principles and the first is this: It is possible to be a modern person and a committed Christian.

Liberals believe that Christianity teaches the truth, a truth just as valid and valuable today as it was in the ancient and medieval worlds. Christianity's basic message does not require belief in a three-layer universe nor is it an outdated relic of a bygone age. The liberal task is to explain Christianity in ways that are clear, relevant and convincing to modern men and women. Working this out in practice remains a continuing challenge.

Our job is as demanding as building the great cathedrals. Paris' Notre Dame cathedral took over 150 years to complete and our own building project has already been underway for some 200 years with no end in sight. Yet if Heinrich Paulus did not complete the job, then David Friedrich Strauss must take up where he left off. If Rudolf Bultmann falters, then another must carry on and another and another. The work may not be finished in our lifetime, or our children's, or our children's children, but the goal can and must be reached.

Nothing Against The Truth

Our second design principle is simple, clear and straightforward. Saint Paul summed it up in his letter to Corinth, "For we cannot do anything against the truth, but only for the truth" (2 Corinthians 13:8 NRSV).

Granted, it is painful when our most sacred and cherished opinions turn out to be false. Copernicus shook the Medieval world when he showed the earth was round and that it moved. Yet our commitment is not to our favorite notions however pious or sincerely held. It is unthinkable that Christians should stand with Pilate when he cynically asks, "What is truth?"

Today, modern society suffocates from dishonesty, deception and deceit. Daily, modern people suffer from the Big Lie, the little lie, the convenient lie, the corporate lie, the political lie, the governmental lie, the advertising lie, the con artist's lie. Addiction specialists assert it is this very lack of truth that fuels addictive behaviors from cocaine users in inner city crack houses to workaholics in downtown corporate board rooms.

In contrast, liberal Christians call for the clear, sparkling word of truth. We seek the truth wherever it leads, whatever the cost. To paraphrase the old Roman maxim, "Speak the truth, though the heavens fall."

FOUR PILLARS OF CHRISTIANITY

There are four liberal beliefs so basic they stand as the pillars of modern Christianity. They are as follows:

A Loving God

First, liberal Christians believe in a loving God who made all that exists and works to bring about creation's fulfillment. God works in nature through the evolutionary process and in history through the human unconscious. Over the ages, humanity and the universe move toward their divinely appointed goal, a destination hidden in the mind of God.

A Crucified Christ

Second, we believe in Jesus Christ, Son of Man and Son of God, Child of Earth and Child of Heaven, the one who symbolizes the inner human. Like him, we are both material and spiritual beings. Through his life, teaching, and most clearly by his death and resurrection, Christ reveals God's suffering love for the world, a love that has existed from the beginning. Meditation upon Christ's passion opens the way for a spiritual awakening and the world's transformation in Christ's image.

God's Revelation In The Bible

Third, Liberal Christianity believes the Bible reveals God's will and speaks meaningfully to modern men and women today. It is inspired by God with an inspiration akin to poetic inspiration rather than dictation to a secretary. As we have seen, its stories must be honored and treasured, told and retold. Often, they must be interpreted symbolically. Some have greater value than others.

In addition, liberals accept the results of modern biblical research. Scholars have shown that many different authors wrote the Bible and, over the centuries, its stories were collected, edited and rearranged.

Further, the Bible does not contain one viewpoint but many. Some biblical passages do contradict others. Yet, these competing views show how the biblical writers' understanding deepened over time as they struggled with their experience and God's will.

Liberals believe the Bible's teaching came to final fulfillment in Christ's cross and resurrection. Therefore, more important than any particular verses are the Bible's great themes including compassion, mercy, forgiveness, sacrifice, moral behavior, justice, peace, trust, hope and love.

Unfortunately, this hardly solves the problem. Like motherhood and apple pie, everyone believes in hope, peace and love. Yet how do these themes apply when deciding real life issues of war and peace? Of euthanasia? Racism? Abortion? Homosexuality?

Everyone believes in justice, but how does this principle guide the church's mission or effect public policy in South Central Los Angeles? All believe in human rights, but in the abortion debate, do we side with the rights of the woman? The unborn? The father? Society? Do we look for a solution that protects, even if imperfectly, the rights of all?

Obviously, these decisions cannot be made easily or lightly no matter what the issue. We look for guidance from scripture and church tradition, from contemporary scholarship and research, from discussion and debate with friends, colleagues, opponents. We listen for a word of inspiration. We weigh consequences. Finally, all must search their conscience and follow their own light.

God's Spirit And World Transformation

Fourth, we believe God's work continues today, gathering a community of believers for support, growth and action. Although God's revelation is complete in Christ's cross and resurrection, our understanding of their meaning is not. Our awareness, knowledge and wisdom continues to grow over time.

Finally, God works both inside and outside the church. As the Bible makes plain, God can and does use both Moses and Pharaoh, both Peter and Judas, to gain divine ends.

MORTAR AND STONE

In this section, we examine Liberal Christianity's mortar and stone. Like the rock quarried for the great cathedrals, the following provide liberal belief's fundamental building blocks.

Freedom And Responsibility

We have seen the cross and resurrection are the most important biblical passages. The second most important is the Exodus.

Moses leading the Israelites from slavery reveals the God who liberates. All people are created to be eternally free; free to think their own thoughts, feel their own feelings, and pursue their own destiny despite race, nation, or gender. As Saint Paul said, "There is no longer Jew or Greek, there is no longer slave or free, there is no longer male or female; for all of you are one in Christ Jesus" (Galatians 3:28 NRSV).

The demand for freedom arises from the fundamental belief that God has a plan for each human life expressed through the unconscious mind. Traditionally, we have called this the "prompting of the Holy Spirit" or, as Quakers put it, "the Inner Light." Therefore, freedom is not license to do anything we please, but the liberty to follow God's inner direction without interference from state authority, social conditions, or accident of birth.

God gives us freedom to accept or reject divine prompting but freedom's potential is not without responsibilities. Consider, for example, the Exodus. Having escaped from Egypt and on their way to the Promised Land, suddenly the Israelites find themselves trapped between Pharaoh's army and the Red Sea. The Book of Exodus records Israel's complaint.

> *They said to Moses, "Was it because there were no graves in Egypt that you have taken us away to die in the wilderness? What have you done to us, bringing us out of Egypt? Is this not the very thing we told you in Egypt, 'Let us alone and let us serve the Egyptians'? For it would have been better for us to serve the Egyptians than to die in the wilderness" (Exodus 14:11-12 NRSV).*

The Israelites did not die at the Red Sea nor during their 40 years of wilderness wanderings. They did, however, continue to complain. Having moved from slavery to freedom, from dependence to independence, they found their new responsibility unnerving. With freedom comes the demand to be responsible for ourselves, to make our own choices and live with the results.

Since the American Revolution, freedom has been an empowering idea of our modern age. Our own century has seen the worldwide rise of liberation movements as people of color in India, China, Africa and Latin America threw off European rule. Although these efforts did bring political freedom, the struggle against economic domination continues. In the United States, the civil rights and women's movements were two key 20th century events whose promise and agendas remain unfulfilled.

Within the church, liberation theology became freedom's most eloquent voice. Black Theology among African Americans, Liberation Theology in Latin America, the Theology of Hope in Europe and Feminist Theology want to align the church with the cause of the oppressed, humiliated and exploited. The goal here is not just to understand the world, but to change it.

In recent years, spirited, sometimes angry, debate has swirled around liberation theology. How these issues should and will be resolved remains an open question.

For liberals, this much is certain: God wills that every person have a good human life. All people should be free to follow their inner light whether white, black, yellow, or red, whether male or female, whether born in the First World or the Third. Within the context of that freedom, all must bear the responsibility for the wisdom or foolishness of their choices. All are created to be eternally free and eternally responsible.

Individual Conscience Before God

Liberal Christianity believes that each person is responsible before God. Final authority, therefore, rests not with the church or the Bible, but with the individual conscience. No one can stand before the divine throne and say, "But our bishop said . . ." or "Our pastor told us that Bible passage meant . . ." We are responsible for ourselves.

Although we have the guidance of inspiration, scripture, tradition and church community, we must seek our own relationship with God. Each must wrestle with his or her own beliefs and moral duty.

But clearly, not everyone does. We can give up our freedom and pretend the bishop, pastor, Bible, or church can tell us what to believe or do. We can surrender our freedom, but we cannot escape our responsibility.

It is important to remember that, as Jung points out, an individual life is Christianity's central symbol. Two biblical passages make this clear. The first comes when Jesus explains to his disciples that he must go to Jerusalem, suffer and die. When Peter objects to this course of action, Jesus is not dissuaded and, in fact, rejects Peter's viewpoint with harsh, even brutal words.

A second passage comes in the Garden of Gethsemane where Jesus prays that, if it is possible, he may escape the cup of suffering. However, he decides to live out his divine mission despite the prospect of a horrible, humiliating death.

In short, central to Christian teaching is that God has been revealed in a single individual. One who follows the divine light despite what others think or what the consequences might be.

Granted, to argue for the individual's importance in modern society seems almost laughable. Society tries to reduce and destroy our humanity at every turn. To corporations, we are not human beings but workers and consumers. To government, we are merely voters and taxpayers. To the media we are no more than viewers condensed into TV ratings. Personal identity is reduced to social security numbers, polling data and electronic markings on computerized bar codes.

As Jung wryly observed, what matters today is mass society, or so it seems. Where the many are is safety. What the many want must be valuable. What the many believe must be true.

Liberal Christianity totally rejects such notions. Salvation, value and truth are not found with the many but with the believer's encounter with God's will. Corporate analysts, government decrees and media moguls do not have ultimate truth's final word. The final decisions will be made, not by mass society, but by God.

What, then, does this mean to the understanding of the church? Simply this. The church is a community made up of those who gather to worship God, love one another, grow spiritually, change society and seek common goals. We choose compromise where possible and respect other's most cherished values. But always, church members reserve the right to follow their conscience before God.

In The Garden Alone?

Yet with that said, the liberal vision is not one of walking with Jesus in the garden alone. We are part of a community including other believers, denominations and churches. We share our different values and viewpoints. We learn from each other and work together; we encourage, argue and debate.

Biblical metaphors of community abound but none is more instructive than Jesus' teaching on prayer. Used so automatically and often, we may easily overlook that the words of the Lord's prayer are plural. *Our* Father . . . give *us* daily bread . . . forgive *us* our debts . . . deliver *us* from evil. Speaking these words we raise our prayers, not just for ourselves, but on behalf of all.

Finally, each must follow his or her conscience, but we are not alone. We belong to an ancient tradition, a worldwide church, a human family, a vast and wondrous creation.

Human Nature

What is human nature like? Perhaps no one in Christian

history took a dimmer view of humans than the Protestant reformer John Calvin. Calvin argued that during the fall in the garden of Eden humanity lost all goodness and potential for goodness. No human act was good without divine help. Every human is in an utter state of complete ruin and deserves only damnation.

The Helvetic Confession written in Switzerland in 1536 put it this way: "We understand original sin to be the native corruption of man which has passed from our first parents to us; through which, being sunk in depraved desires, averse to good, inclined to evil, full of every wickedness, of contempt and hatred of God, we are unable to do or even to think any good whatever."

The liberal theologians of the late 19th and early 20th century rejected Calvin's opinion, taking a positive view of human nature. Influenced by the great progress in science and industry, they believed humans were basically good and were making moral progress. We were getting better and better, everyday in every way. Sin could be eliminated by force of will, or so they believed.

World War I changed all that. Humanity in general and liberal scholars in particular could not help but learn a lesson from 10,000,000 deaths in European trenches. The endless rows of grave markers made the human potential for evil all too clear.

If one lesson had not been enough, just 20 years later it was reinforced by another global war. Germany, the most advanced and civilized European power, dropped into the depths of paganism and plunged the world into another nightmare of fire and blood.

As a result, liberals developed a more realistic view of human nature. Sin and human evil cannot be wished away. Human beings are capable of great good, but are inclined toward evil. There is within the human heart potential for great compassion, courage and integrity. Yet, given the right circumstances and motivation, we are also capable of unimaginable evil no matter how mild and peaceful we might appear to be.

A Social Gospel

In the gospels, Jesus' deep concern for human suffering is clear. Liberal Christianity teaches, therefore, that each believer must share that concern for human well being, both in this world and the next.

In Luke and Matthew's gospels we find two key passages. First, Luke tells us Jesus began his ministry in his hometown synagogue where he read from the book of Isaiah:

> *The Spirit of the Lord is upon me,*
> *because he has anointed me to bring good news to the poor.*
> *He has sent me to proclaim release to captives*
> *and recovery of sight to the blind,*
> *to let the oppressed go free,*
> *to proclaim the year of the Lord's favor" (Luke 4:18-19 NRSV).*

With all eyes fixed upon him, Jesus states this scripture has come true while the congregation has been listening.

A second important passage comes in Matthew's 25th chapter. Here, Jesus pictures the Great Judgment when all the world's nations will stand before the divine throne. Their eternal destinies will be decided by whether they have fed the hungry, welcomed the stranger, clothed the naked, cared for the sick and visited those in prison.

Liberals see in these passages, and others like them, that basic to Jesus' ministry was concern for the poor, sick, captive and oppressed. The nations will be judged by how they treat those in need.

Liberals also look to the Old Testament prophet's call for social justice. The prophet Amos makes plain that God wants justice more than correct worship or ritual purity.

> *Take away from me the noise of your songs;*
> *I will not listen to the melody of your harps.*
> *But let justice roll down like waters,*
> *and righteousness like an everflowing stream*
> *(Amos 5:23-24 NRSV).*

Around the turn of the 20th century, liberals realized the industrial revolution had brought a great advance in material wealth but had also created a laboring class treated with less concern than machines and animals. To provide even the most meager living, many men, women, and often children, worked 15 hours a day, seven days a week. Industrial accidents killed and injured thousands every year, injuries that could have been easily prevented by modest safety precautions.

And yet, while the many labored in dangerous, inhuman conditions, a few industrialists lived beyond medieval kings' wildest dreams of avarice, comfort and splendor. Liberal Christians believed the current social situation was an intolerable offense to a God who demanded justice roll like a river and righteousness like an everflowing stream.

A key leader of this new "social gospel" movement was Walter Rauschenbusch (1861-1918). A seminary professor in Rochester, New York, Rauschenbusch saw the enormous and growing gap between the rich and poor. He recognized that religion could hardly be important to those struggling daily to provide life's most basic needs. Even worse, he saw a middle class church unwilling to challenge upper class power and privilege.

Rauschenbusch argued the church must teach the individual soul is worth more than material things and society must value people above profits. Sin exists in economic organizations as surely as in human hearts. Christians must align with the poor and oppressed as their Lord had done.

Rauschenbusch was not alone. The concern for society's sins cut across denominational lines and included Protestants, Roman Catholics and Jews. Religious leaders like James Cardinal Gibbons (1834-1921) came to the defense of labor unions. He warned the Catholic church that it could not force the faithful to choose between being good Catholics and good union men and women.

Jane Addams (1860-1935), following her Quaker father's teaching, argued the church must be present in the tenements and slums. She pointed out the Lord had not brought his lunch with him and returned to heaven at night. Her Hull House, and other tenement houses like it, became oases of hope in barren urban communities, providing spiritual life, education, culture, entertainment, financial help and medical care.

Rabbi Samuel S. Mayerberg (1892-1964) took on the political corruption of Kansas City, Missouri. He attacked a system that violated human dignity and dominated both the city's public and private life. Despite his phone being tapped, his office ransacked, harassment and threats, he continued to struggle for change.

Since the social gospel's beginning, old issues have not disappeared and new ones have been added. Many problems press for attention including racism, women's issues, child abuse, health care, hunger and homelessness to name a few.

There are global issues as well. Television has brought painful images into our living rooms from Ethiopia to Bangladesh. Videos of starving children covered with flies symbolize the ever widening gap between the First World and the Third. Added to these, Jurgen Moltmann suggests there are really only two issues: overpopulation and ecology. If these problems are not solved, no others will matter.

Simply put, Liberal Christianity cares about people's lives in this time, in this world. Never in history have the stakes been as high, and as always, the harvest is heavy and laborers are few. All must make their contribution to the world's well being.

Human Dignity

Liberals believe that every person, created in God's image, a little lower than the angels, deserves the chance for a good life and to be treated with dignity. As Martin Luther King, Jr., noted, all people should be judged by the content of their character not by their race, nationality, sex, age, economic status, or other accidents of birth.

Every child deserves the chance for a decent life: for love, food, shelter, medical care, education, meaningful work and self expression.

Equally, we are all responsible for our actions and choices. Each should contribute in proportion to his or her abilities to the well-being of others and society. Much is required of those to whom much is given.

Moral Behavior

In a world awash in violence, crime and contempt for others, Liberal Christianity teaches believers should act morally and take responsibility for their lives. All should cultivate the traditional moral virtues of temperance, prudence, justice, courage and wisdom.

Here, temperance is the ability to control our passions. Prudence considers the consequences of our actions. Justice means treating others fairly and, when necessary, being willing to endure injustice. Courage is the willingness to suffer pain to gain some good that can be gotten in no other way. Finally, wisdom means the ability to learn from our experience.

To those traditional moral virtues, liberals add the religious virtues of trust, hope and love.

Liberals look to the three great sources of Christian and Western ethics as the basic guides for individual behavior — the Ten Commandments, the Golden Rule and Jesus' commandment "Love one another as I have loved you."

Tolerance

Basic to Liberal Christianity is a tolerant attitude toward other Christian denominations, world religions, and those of different cultural, national and racial backgrounds. Tolerance is rooted in Jesus' own compassion found in biblical passages like "Do not judge, and you will not be judged; do not condemn, and you will not be condemned. Forgive, and you will be forgiven . . ." (Luke 6:37 NRSV).

Christian history makes tolerance especially important. Looking back, it is sometimes hard to remember that Jesus taught love for God, neighbor and even enemies. Through the centuries, Christians have been more likely to kill enemies than to love them.

For example, Luther's Reformation did open the way for a mighty surge of Bible study but this new emphasis brought neither peace nor unity. In Switzerland, Ulrich Zwingli and John Calvin used Luther's methods but came to different conclusions. Even more disturbing was a loosely knit group known as the Anabaptists who followed Luther's guideline that every doctrine and ritual should be measured against the Bible's authority. Unable to find support for infant baptism, they ended the practice. Converts received "believer's baptism," hence the name Anabaptists or "rebaptizers."

The Lutheran camp had not foreseen anything like this. It soon became clear the process they had set in motion would be easier to start than to control or stop.

Debate over the Bible's interpretation aroused deep passions that quickly moved from scholarly research, to angry debate, to outright violence. For example, during the early 16th century the peasants' condition in central and southwestern Germany was pitiful and growing steadily worse. With leadership from radicals like Thomas Muntzer, the peasants mixed their social agenda with biblical prophecies predicting a new age of abundance. When their pleas for social justice were ignored, and spurred on by the Reformation's rebellious spirit, the movement turned to violence.

At first, Luther felt some sympathy for the peasants' plight. But as violent disorder grew, Luther, the revolutionary, found himself cast in the role of the establishment's defender. He wrote a pamphlet, *Against the Murderous and Thieving Rabble of the Peasants*, calling on Germany's princes to crush the rebellion without mercy. They did exactly that in a wild orgy of slaughter that left 100,000 dead.

The Peasant's Rebellion was only the beginning. Soon Catholic would be pitted against Protestant, Protestant against Catholic, all against the Anabaptists. Religious conflict sparked what became known as the Thirty Year's War in which Spain, France and Sweden with the aide of German princes fought across German soil. By the war's end in 1648, much of Germany's landscape was a smoldering ruins.

For liberals, using the Bible as a weapon of bigotry and hatred is intolerable. Any church teaching that justifies the poor's oppression or the persecution of others just for holding different views is hardly the teaching of Christ.

Is Mahatma Gandhi Burning In Hell?

A second important question is the Christian attitude toward other world religions. Clearly, Christianity makes what seems an exclusive claim. Namely, among the world's religions only we have the complete truth. It is our Jesus who is the Christ. Our Bible reveals the true God. We are the ones instructed to proclaim the good news to all the world.

Yet what if, as has so often happened in Christian history, the good news becomes the profoundly bad news of arrogance, contempt, persecution, torture and even genocide? Can such attitudes be held, can such actions be taken in the name of a humble carpenter from Nazareth who taught love for God and neighbor? Unquestionably, the liberal answer is "No."

Liberals return to the cross and resurrection for instruction. In light of God's suffering love revealed in Christ's death, liberals ask we take a humble, loving attitude toward all people whether Jew, Buddhist, Hindu or Moslem. Here, compassion for people takes precedence over concern for correct ideas.

As Paul states in the 13th chapter of 1 Corinthians, love is not boastful or arrogant or rude. It does not insist on its own way. Without love, all the precisely correct doctrine in the world is no more than a noisy gong or a clanging cymbal and often much worse.

Granted, in John's gospel Jesus states, ". . . I am the way, and the truth, and the life. No one comes to the Father except through me" (John 14:6 NRSV). But what does such a statement mean? How do we come to God through a humiliated, beaten and crucified savior?

Liberals contend we approach God through divine grace, not by speaking certain words nor by holding certain beliefs. We respond by trust in God's love for all people. We grow through a resurrection process of life, death and rebirth. We seek to live with a heart of compassion, mercy and forgiveness. Perhaps for once Christians can interpret such passages symbolically and avoid the arrogance and contempt that has haunted our history for so long.

Tolerant Of Intolerance?

Yet, the liberal idea of tolerance clearly brings its own set of problems. Can liberals be tolerant of intolerance?

Without doubt, there are powerful and determined religious and political forces on the left and right who would gladly force their rigidly intolerant views on both the church and all society. Can liberal institutions defend themselves from the intolerant without destroying both freedom and compassion? Or, will liberals simply hand over the keys to our institutions? Will we give in to those who would seize control of humane Western traditions and turn them to their narrow minded and authoritarian agendas? How these issues can and should be resolved remains a critical question for the liberal church.

Democratic Government

Liberals believe God speaks to each heart and that the divine will expresses itself through God's people rather than a religious or political hierarchy. Therefore, church organization must be democratic.

Separation Of Church And State

Liberals take the separation of church and state for granted. Because each individual must be free to respond to God's will, the state has no right to interfere with an individual's beliefs or the practice of his or her religion. Equally, no religion, church or denomination has the right to force its beliefs and practices on others by threat of government power. Nor should any church be supported by the public treasury.

With that said, liberals also believe churches and individuals can and, in fact, have a responsibility, to help shape government policy on their day's important issues. Christian values have a crucial role in public life. Deciding which values are most pressing and how they should be put into action remains an on-going challenge. Generally, liberals tend to see their role as advocates for the poor and disadvantaged rather than trying to advance their particular church or denomination.

In contrast, some conservative churches lobby for required Christian prayer, Bible reading in public schools and nativity scenes displayed on public property. Conservatives see the end of government supported Christian rituals and symbols as evidence of American society's collapse. Some even call for creating a "Christian commonwealth." One trembles to think how far such groups, if given a free hand, might go toward enforcing an official government religion. One wonders if they believe in separation of church and state at all.

The Possibility Of Progress

Liberal Christians have always believed in progress. Granted, in 1900 that belief was too optimistic and naive. However, the 20th century's horrors have been a sobering experience. Liberals know that progress does not run in a straight line ever upward. Real evil exists in the world and often wins. Injustices do occur. Sin and evil cannot be wished away.

Yet in spite of the world's evil, God works to bring creation's fulfillment and aims toward the good. Universal justice is slow but certain. Rooted in the divine plan, progress is possible. In fact, it is inevitable.

In addition, liberals believe progress is also possible in religious life and thought. Christianity is a living relationship with God, and therefore, can continue to develop and deepen over time. God's revelation in Christ's cross and resurrection is complete but our understanding of its meaning and implications is not. Further, situations change. New tasks challenge us and new insights are given. Therefore, we remain open to change and the future God envisions.

SUMMARY

As the great cathedrals were rising, little villages grew up around the construction site, providing housing for the professional stone masons, carpenters and artisans who came to build the church. Yet entire towns also gave both their money and labor. Without the effort of hundreds, the great cathedral's towers would never have reached the sky. In the truest sense, they were community projects.

Liberal Christian belief is a community project too. In this chapter I have tried to lay out what I consider basics. Perhaps you think I gave too much emphasis to some topics, not enough to others and ignored what are burning issues for you.

Let me say in self defense, my concern here is with fundamentals, not particulars. For example, human dignity is fundamental but has many applications. The American Civil Rights movement which energized the liberal church in the 1960s was based on belief in human dignity. In the 1990s we might add concerns like women's rights, racism, concern for AIDS victims, and on and on. Yet concern for human dignity underlies them all.

But perhaps you still think my list is all wrong and want to create your own. If so, welcome to the conversation.

Chapter 7

BRIDGE THE HUMAN RIFT

Gaining The World . . .

When Abbot Suger and his Medieval friends walked through Saint-Denis' doors, they entered a mystical realm suspended between heaven and earth. They walked on holy ground in the light of divine essence. Theirs was a small comfortable world where spiritual paths were well marked. Clearly, that is no longer true today.

Without doubt, the modern world has given us much. But now, guided again by Jung's observations, we see what it has taken away. Consider, for example, the isolated primitive tribes that survived into the 20th century living just as they did 4,000 years ago. What happened when modern civilization and these ancient peoples came into contact? Almost invariably their primitive society collapsed. Within a few short years, they became the modern world's apathetic, addicted and hopeless wards.

Why is this so? Jung found the answer traveling in the American West during the early 20th century. On his visit, he learned about the Pueblo's ancient religion and found that each morning they performed their sacred mysteries, convinced this would help Father Sun cross the sky. And if they stopped? In that case, Father Sun would have more and more trouble until finally, he would be unable to cross the sky at all. Then, the earth would grow dark and every living thing would die.

Of course, moderns smile at such nonsense. We know the earth's rotation causes the sun to rise and set. It will continue to do so whether rituals are performed or not. Yet what a terrible price we have paid for that bit of information.

Consider the difference between modern and primitive daily life. Primitives arose each morning confident their efforts were vital to their well being, their community, the earth, and even the gods themselves. We moderns arise to fill our places in a vast industrial complex knowing that in the event of our absence, we can, must, and will be quickly replaced. We know the earth will spin, the sun rise and set, no matter what we do, no matter whether we live or die.

. . . And Losing Our Souls

In contrast to our primitive relatives, we live in an impersonal world. Our presence has little importance and sometimes it seems our absence might actually be preferred. Society gives little or no spiritual guidance. We have much information but little wisdom. Technological power, but little virtue. Material comfort but spiritual poverty. We have gained the world but have lost our souls.

Like Adam and Eve, we have been thrust from the garden of innocence. An angel with a flaming sword bars our return to childish faith in Abbot Suger's three-layer world with all its supernatural beings and events. And yet, we cannot live human lives in a spiritual wasteland.

Clearly, we know more than primitives. But what we do not so easily recognize is this. We have gone through exactly the same wrenching changes that drive newly discovered primitive tribes to desperation and despair. Although moderns have had centuries to adjust, the effects have been no less jarring to our psychological, emotional and spiritual well being.

How, then, can we regain our spiritual bearings? Not in a tranquil three-layer world, but on a small planet racing through the universe at enormous speeds. How can we recover our souls? This, Jung notes, is the supreme challenge of our time.

Today no one can answer that question. The world moves now through a great spiritual transformation. As Jung states, we live in what the Greeks called "the right time" for a "metamorphosis of the gods," that is, a fundamental shift of symbols and principles. The outcome of this transformation is unknown. Whether humanity will even survive it, is far from certain. Nor are we directing this movement by conscious will. The modern world's great spiritual struggle will be solved for us, not by us.

Yet now is the time when we must live, decide and act. How do we live during this "in between" time? The remainder of this chapter suggests a possibility.

IN SEARCH OF A SOUL

8 Points And 12 Steps

In 1908, Frank Buchman, a Lutheran minister from Philadelphia, was on a spiritual pilgrimage to the English Lake country. Here, he experienced a life transforming moment while attending a worship service in a small church near Keswick village. From this experience, Buchman developed the

Oxford Group to bring Christianity to college students. So named because its first leaders were recruited from Oxford University, its spiritual method included 8 points. In the following decades, it spread to 48 countries across the world.

In the 1930s, the budding Alcoholics Anonymous movement adapted the 8 Points for their purposes. Although the Oxford Group died out, its spiritual method lived on in AA's 12 Steps and continues to be a powerful force worldwide.

With the Oxford Group's end, the 8 Points moved into church basements where so many AA groups have met ever since. I suggest liberal churches need to bring this tradition up from the basement and return it to a central place in church life.

What do the 8 Points offer the liberal church today? First, AA and other recovery groups have shown this method has real power. Second, whether called the 8 Points, the 12 Steps or another name, it grows from Christianity's historic understanding of spiritual life. Third, it offers a reasonable approach suited to modern men and women that can be practiced by anyone. It does not require a seminary degree nor retreat to a monastery to follow its methods. Finally, the church needs an easily understood, straightforward way to help people grow spiritually and to strengthen the church's community life.

Bookstores are flooded with recovery books adapting the 12 Steps to problems ranging from eating disorders to codependency. Any of these may give useful information about 12 Steps and often give personal testimony of God's power. Further, in 1992, Stephen Arterburn and David Stoop published *The Life Recovery Bible* that applies 12 Step principles to biblical stories, characters and passages. Although its main focus is recovery, it is an excellent work for anyone.

The following lists the original 8 Points and its adaptation by Alcoholics Anonymous.

Bridge The Human Rift

The 8 Points	The 12 Steps
1. Surrender to God	1. We admitted we were powerless over Alcohol — that our lives had become unmanageable. 2. Came to believe that a Power greater than ourselves could restore us to sanity. 3. Made a decision to turn our will and our lives over to the care of God *as we understood Him.*
2. Confession/Sharing	4. Made a searching and fearless moral inventory of ourselves. 5. Admitted to God, to ourselves and to another human being the exact nature of our wrongs. 6. Were entirely ready to have God remove all these defects of character. 7. Humbly asked Him to remove all our shortcomings.
3. Restitution	8. Made a list of all persons we had harmed, and became willing to make amends to them all. 9. Made direct amends to such people wherever possible, except when to do so would injure them or others.
4. Daily Checking	10. Continued to take personal inventory and when we were wrong promptly admitted it.
5. The Quiet Time 6. Guidance	11. Sought through prayer and meditation to improve our conscious contact with God, *as we understood Him*, praying only for knowledge of His will for us and the power to carry it out.
7. Witness 8. Fellowship	12. Having a spiritual awakening as the results of these steps, we tried to carry this message to alcoholics, and to practice these principles in all our affairs. *(See copyright page.)

PRINCIPLES

In this section, we briefly examine the principles that underlie both the 8 Points and the 12 Steps.

Surrender To God

The spiritual journey begins with the realization that we are not God. Perhaps, looking up at a glittering night sky, we grasp, for the first time, the awesome size and mystery of the universe in which we live. Or suddenly, all our carefully made future plans are changed forever by an unexpected event. Or, an overpowering inner compulsion turns our lives in new and totally unforeseen directions.

Confronting the mysteries of the universe and existence, of fate and destiny, we experience the simple truth. We are part of something bigger than ourselves. Something more directs our lives than conscious will. There are some things we cannot control.

Once realizing a Higher Power exists, we must ask, "What is it like?" Is the power behind the universe friendly and trustworthy? Is it evil and out to kill us? Is the universe completely neutral? Perhaps, it is unaware that it has made us and does not care.

As we have seen, Abelard argued that contemplating Christ's death we find the answer to these questions. Upon the cross, we see God's loving attitude toward us from the beginning. We see a God who seeks creation's fulfillment and offers to all humanity power, pardon and purpose.

And so, having come to believe the universe is loving and dependable, we make a leap of faith. We make an intentional decision to respond, giving our trust and loyalty to God. We seek to surrender our little will to the Divine Will. Admitting our dependence, we find our proper relationship to life's source.

Inner peace comes as we accept our place in the universe and our role in it. The great liberal scholar Reinhold Niebuhr provided us with a now world-famous prayer. "O God, grant me the serenity to accept the things I cannot change, the courage to change the things I can, and the wisdom to know the difference."

We are not God, but neither are we worms. Some things in this world can be changed by human effort, some cannot. Each of us has the power to do some things but not all things. We do what we can and pray, "Thy will be done."

Confession

Arguing that only God could forgive sins, the Protestant Reformation abolished private confession. It was good theology but terrible psychology. Once having slammed the confessional's door, Protestants were left alone with their sin. Yet guilt still weighed heavy as both a spiritual and psychological problem. It seems Roman Catholics may now suffer the same fate as confession is "modernized" and becomes more like counseling.

I once asked two friends about their experience of private confession, brothers who grew up in an Italian Roman Catholic family. One said it offered nothing and he went only to please his parents. With that, his brother's eyes opened wide in disbelief. In contrast, he described the enormous sense of relief he felt, as if the slate had been wiped clean and a great weight lifted.

Admittedly, "sometimes the magic works and sometimes it doesn't." Yet there can be little doubt the burden of unresolved guilt and shame continues growing across the modern world.

Both the 8 Points and the 12 Steps understand that confession's dynamics are essential. Like the Oxford movement,

AA continues to use group confession but the 12 Steps takes a slightly different approach. Steps 4 and 5 tell us to make a "fearless moral inventory" and to confess the "exact nature of our wrongs" to God, ourselves and another human being.

Admittedly, there are difficulties. Whether in a group or to another individual, confession requires a high level of trust and compassion. There are pitfalls working out this tenet in practice but the problems are not as great as living in an increasingly guilt-ridden and shame-burdened world.

James' letter in the New Testament states, "Therefore confess your sins to one another, and pray for one another, so that you may be healed" (James 5:16 NRSV). As James suggests, in confession we confront the past and our moral failings to find forgiveness and healing. Our modern world needs few things more.

Restitution

Restitution means we make amends to those we have hurt. Traditionally, the church has called this penance. We make up for what we have done wrong. However, we do so only if making restitution will not hurt others again. The purpose is to correct old wrongs, not make ourselves feel better at another's expense.

The spiritual life begins as we give our lives to God's care. It continues with confession and restitution.

Daily Checking

Daily checking helps keep us on track.

Contemplation

The gospel's story of Mary and Martha suggest two ways of being in the world.

Now as they went on their way, he entered a certain village, where a woman named Martha welcomed him into her home. She had a sister named Mary, who sat at the Lord's feet and listened to what he was saying. But Martha was distracted by her many tasks; so she came to him and asked, 'Lord, do you not care that my sister has left me to do all the work by myself? Tell her then to help me.' But the Lord answered her, 'Martha, Martha, you are worried and distracted by so many things; there is need for only one thing. Mary has chosen the better part, which will not be taken away from her' (Luke 10:38-42 NRSV).

Modern society values useful people and things; we feel compelled to be productive. Like Martha, we are busy with so many tasks, the busier the better. We have an endless array of time-saving devices yet so little time.

But what is the purpose of all the rushing, efficiency and achievement if life's wonders can never be enjoyed? Every day on my way to the office I drive past a small pond that is home to a flock of Canadian geese. Often, as the morning sun reddens the sky over Pennsylvania's hills, I want to stop and just spend a few minutes watching the geese, yet I never do. There is no time.

Mary's more contemplative approach says, "Stop and be." There is need for one thing only. We have as much right to be here as the oceans and trees.

Guidance

Both the 8 Points and the 12 Steps teach that God has a plan for our lives, a plan that we can come to know and follow. We seek God's guidance, or as Quakers put it, the "Inner Light."

How can we know this plan? Joseph Campbell told his students "follow your bliss." We find God's will for our lives by following what, in our heart of hearts, makes us happiest and what we want most to do.

Henry Drummond wrote on the flyleaf of his Bible a way to know God's will that is as helpful as any. "First, pray; second, think; third, talk to wise people, but don't regard their judgment as final. Fourth, beware of the objection of your own will, but don't be too much afraid of it. God never unnecessarily thwarts a man's nature and likings; it is a mistake to think that His will is always in the line of the disagreeable. Fifth, meanwhile do the next thing, for doing God's will in small things is the best preparation for doing it in great things. Sixth, when decision and action are necessary, go ahead. Seventh, you will probably not find out until afterwards, perhaps long afterwards, that you have been led at all."

Witness

For the Oxford Groups, witness aimed at changing individuals as one person shared their experience with another. Yet, Liberal Christianity sees wider implications. There are many ways to witness; God gives different tasks to different people.

As my Baptist friends might ask, "What burden is the Lord laying on your heart?" My task may not be yours, but all can express their love for God. Perhaps your task is to share your faith's meaning with a neighbor or support an orphanage in El Salvador. For someone else, it may be sitting in silence with a young man whose brother has just committed suicide. Or delivering meals on wheels. Or lobbying congress about a burning issue. Or running for congress. Whatever the task, all can and must make their contributions to build temples still undone.

Community

Both the Oxford Group and Alcoholics Anonymous stress

building human relationships and rightly so. As the modern pace of change quickens, we lose our connection with people and place.

For example, my paternal family's baptismal records go back to 1698 in one Lutheran church in Adolzhausen, Germany. The Flurers lived in that village for over 200 years until my grandfather left for London in 1908. Yet like many modern people, my own life has been constant movement, having lived in six towns and cities in the past 25 years. The situation for modern men and women evokes biblical images of homeless wanderers, of strangers in a strange land.

Even if we live in the same place all our lives, we cannot stop the world from changing around us. When I return to the town where I grew up, now 25 years later, I hardly recognize it. Roads have been rerouted; new traffic lights and stop signs seem to spring from the ground; familiar buildings have been torn down, new ones built. Childhood friends have left to travel paths around the country and the world.

More than ever, churches must be oases of friendship and community in an impersonal world.

SUMMARY

In this chapter, my purpose has been to identify the modern world's most critical spiritual crisis and suggest a possible solution with broad brush strokes. To do more would mean turning this chapter into a thick book or many books. Like friends and colleagues who attend AA, I agree the 12 Steps is today's most vital spiritual path, yet it is clearly not the definitive answer to the modern quest. The world's great spiritual transformation is far from over.

Instead, this chapter is in the spirit of a Medieval pilgrim walking Europe's roads to visit the great cathedrals. I offer it, not as a final answer, but as one beggar tells another where a little bread for the journey might be found.

Chapter 8

WE BUILD WITH THEE

Seeds Of Renewal

During World War II, an English church was preparing for its yearly harvest celebration. By Saturday night, the sanctuary's altar had been decorated with the autumn's fruits, vegetables and grain. Everything was ready for the following morning's worship. That night, however, two Nazi bombs came crashing through the church roof and exploded, collapsing the building. Only rubble remained. A long difficult winter followed. But the next spring, neighbors noticed a vigorous patch of wheat growing out of the rubble where the altar had stood.

Like this English church, we have seen Saint-Denis reduced to a ruined pile of glass and stone by the forces that built the modern world. Yet we have also found that Christianity contains within itself the seeds of renewal. We have discovered science and Christianity are compatible. That the Bible's vision remains crucial to modern men and women. That fundamental to the teaching of the prophets and Jesus was a concern for people's needs and suffering, in this time, in this world. The Medieval world is gone, but Christianity's essential message lives on.

A POWERFUL VISION

Liberal Christianity has a mighty vision, yet it cannot survive unless embodied in dynamic churches, organizations and institutions. Equally, Mainline denominations will not survive if we address the 16th century's needs rather than those of the 21st. Even if foundations can be rebuilt, walls raised and windows remade, what can a new Saint-Denis offer the modern world?

A Reason To Hope

First, Liberal Christianity offers our world's best hope. Thinking back on all we have seen, who's vision should shape the future? Would we prefer the Ayatollah Khomeini's plan for a good society? Or perhaps Christian fundamentalism? Or Madison Avenue's seductive materialism? Wall Street's privilege and wealth? Darth Vader's technologically sophisticated terror?

Where else can we turn? Other than Liberal Christianity, what can keep us from falling into utter despair? What other approach can tackle the enormous challenges facing humanity and our planet without, as T. S. Elliot might say, ending the world with a bang or a whimper?

In contrast to authoritarian and materialistic alternatives, Liberal Christianity looks to a spiritual rebirth of compassion, freedom and ecological sanity. It trusts God who works through evolution and the unconscious to gain divine goals. The Christian's task is to align with this glorious cause. That is the future's hope.

A Dynamic Faith

Second, Liberal Christianity offers a dynamic tradition of faith. Trust in a loving, living God and a crucified Christ. A commitment to individual conscience, freedom, responsibility and truth. A passionate concern for human dignity, justice, peace, community and the social gospel. A belief in moral behavior, tolerance, the possibility of progress, democratic government, the separation of church and state.

It is possible to be modern and Christian. We can accept science's findings, be enriched by the cultural advances of the last 500 years, enjoy technology's benefits and be people of faith.

A Place To Be

Third, in a cold, hard modern world, a new Saint-Denis can be a sanctuary in the truest sense. A place where we find the solid rock of God's love. A place of friendship, comfort and refuge where we can reach across racial and class lines. A place to find the essentially human that binds us together in spite of our differences.

A Rich Tradition

Fourth, we can offer spiritual direction to men and women fallen prey to the emptiness of materialism and greed. We have an enormously rich tradition and, like the householder in Jesus' parable, we can draw both old and new from our storeroom.

As we have seen, the 8 Points/12 Steps can be returned to a central place in the church. In addition, much more is available. Catholic spirituality, Protestant piety, Quaker contemplation, Jungian psychology and other modern psychological approaches can help guide us through the modern world's spiritual wasteland.

A Compelling Mission

Fifth, we can and must challenge people both inside and outside the church to help solve the enormous and complex problems facing our world. One hardly needs to catalog them again. As Moltmann has pointed out, overpopulation and ecology are the most critical concerns. If these problems are not solved, poverty, racism, education, economic development, health care and all the rest will not matter.

Yet plainly, there is no shortage of issues for churches to tackle. From the spiritual concerns of Bible and belief, to the material ones of hunger and homelessness, we have our marching orders: to go, do, heal, teach, make disciples, transform the world.

A Global Impact

Finally, located in North America at the world's power center, the Mainline church's role is both critical and unique. What we do will impact all humankind. Let me explain exactly what I mean.

In his book, *Out of Control*, former national security advisor Zbigniew Brzezinski makes a surprising argument for a foreign policy expert. Brzezinski maintains that the United States' future on the world scene depends in large part on our spiritual values.

Since the Soviet Union's fall, America stands supreme as the world's only remaining superpower. Only the United States can project military force anywhere in the world. Although facing a long list of economic and social ills, we remain the world's largest economy. Most of these troubles, Brzezinski argues, can be dealt with directly and successfully. In fact, we are already beginning to do so.

Yet a more serious and troubling challenge remains. America's leadership role depends on more than military and economic might. Every great superpower also must have a relevant message for the world. It must be an example of "the good society."

Clearly, the world's developing nations would like to copy America's economic success. Yet our voracious appetite for instant gratification, consumption, violence and sex is robbing us of our moral authority and leadership. Nations look to us and say, "We want the things you have, but we do not want your values."

America's position as the world's leader is being undercut and could finally be lost because of our spiritual poverty. And, unfortunately, this problem cannot be so easily solved.

What would be the consequences of such a loss? If America falters, Brzezinski argues convincingly that neither Japan nor Europe could fill the world's leadership vacuum. The result would be increasing global instability. Peaceful change would become violent conflict. The world would head down a slippery slope toward chaos.

Brzezinski also points out that Russia, Eastern Europe and Third World nations need more than economic help to become modern democratic societies. Although adopting democratic forms, they have no liberal traditions on which to build.

Who better to spread that tradition than the liberal, Mainline church? In fact, who else can? Who else has a broad, liberal tradition of spirituality, freedom, human dignity, tolerance, social justice and democratic government?

A great deal rides on the Mainline church's future and on the actions we are about to take. Far more is at stake than the fate of a few congregations. We must now find ways to press our agenda and advance our vision. We must revive the spiritual life of our churches, neighborhoods and nation. For if we fail, America may well lead the world into a new Dark Age from which humanity and the earth may never recover.

A DAUNTING TASK

Now I want to switch gears. I want to move from the global and visionary to the local and practical. From the coolly reasonable to the intensely personal. Now, I want to engage you directly in conversation.

As I type these words, I wonder who you are and what motivates you. Considering you have read this far, I can guess you are a serious-minded person, someone deeply committed to the Christian cause and to your church. Your Christian commitment means a great deal, more than you can put into words. I trust that, like me, you are worried about the Mainline Church.

Perhaps your main concern is your local congregation. Over the years, you've watched it slowly decline. The young disappear after high school, never to return. Those who remain are older and grayer. Giving is down. The Sunday school, nearly empty. You fear what the future holds.

Some years ago, your church began focusing on survival rather than mission. The more numbers fell, the further mission was pushed into the background. Slowly, you have watched your church's vitality sapped. Its energy wane; its enthusiasm die.

On the other hand, perhaps your congregation is doing well. Membership grows modestly or at least holds its own every year. Money is never really a problem. And yet, something is missing. You want a more powerful and relevant message. Deeper spiritual growth. A more vital community. A more passionate concern for mission.

You are also painfully aware that many other congregations are in deep trouble. Each year you read the articles in *Newsweek* and *Time* magazines detailing Mainline losses. You are saddened by headlines like "Dead End for the Mainline Church?" and "The Mainline Moves To the Sideline."

You realize that across America all the Mainline denominations are suffering. Numbers and giving continue to slip. Fewer enter the clergy. The voices of prominent liberal Christian leaders have disappeared from the national scene. Like fundamentalists after the Scopes Monkey trial, it seems that the Mainline church will be forever relegated to the backwaters of American life.

Perhaps you serve in professional ministry as a pastor with responsibility for a local church. Or, maybe you are a denominational executive with responsibility for many churches. The church is your life's work. You feel deep disappointment, frustration and anger about what's happening. To paraphrase Winston Churchill, you did not become an ordained minister to preside over the dissolution of the Mainline church.

Despite the details, something within us both has brought us a long way together. Now I want to ask you directly for your help. Rebuilding is possible. Yet, the task is so daunting, the need so great, the stakes so high, we need all the help we can get.

I want you to use your influence whether in a local congregation, seminary, conference, diocese or synod. I want you to bring your skills to bear. Perhaps you alone can strike the spark that begins renewal in your church.

So, if you have dreamed of what your church might be, then perhaps we can dream together. If you have wondered what could be done, perhaps we can plan together. If you are ready to act, perhaps, together, we can do something new and beautiful for God.

A WORLD OF NEED

By now, I hope you are wondering how your church can embody the liberal Christian vision. How it can be a beacon of hope, comfort and challenge to your community and world. I suggest you start by looking out your church door. A world of need lies beyond our walls.

Psychologist Abraham Maslow offers a helpful framework to consider what might be done. Maslow suggests that human needs are arranged like a ladder. Needs on the lower rungs must be met before we can move to higher ones. They are as follows:

Self Actualization
Self Worth
Love and Belonging
Safety
Physical Needs

For example, a homeless woman wandering New York City's streets must spend her energy meeting basic physical needs. Today, she must find enough food, warmth and shelter to survive until tomorrow. While hungry, dirty and shivering, she will have little time or energy to contemplate life's meaning.

However, consider a college professor with her doctorate in physics, a happy marriage, two bright children, food in the freezer, some money in the bank and a home on a tree-lined street. Returning from delivering a lecture at a scientific conference, she may unexpectedly find herself sitting on the plane thinking about God and existence, about truth and justice, about the meaning and purpose of her life.

In other words, until more elemental needs are met, we are not free to move to higher, spiritual ones. Now we examine each level, with attention to how churches might respond.

Physical Needs

Every person needs food, shelter, warmth and sleep, the basics for biological survival. Dating back to Saint Stephen in the Book of Acts, the church has a long tradition of concern for the physical needs of the poor, sick, old and children. It was the social gospel's founder, Walter Rauschenbusch, who realized decades ago that those laboring in factories or coal mines 15 hours a day did not have energy to worry about religion.

Looking out your church door, what pressing physical needs can you see? Even if located in a wealthy suburb, you need not look far. From the local food pantry to homeless shelters, from hospice care to the widening gap between rich and poor, there is no end of needs to address.

Perhaps your church might create "mission action groups." For example, a group to help elderly folk repair the house and car. One to swing hammers for Habitat for Humanity. Another to support an orphanage in Eastern Europe or El Salvador. A group to deliver meals on wheels and run errands for shut-ins. Any congregation can find plenty to do.

Safety

Once basic biological needs are satisfactorily met, we move up to the next rung, physical security. We all need to feel safe and be protected from harm.

In recent years, violent crime has pushed its way into the national media spotlight. Let me give you a personal example of what I mean. A few years ago I drove on to the campus at Bethany Children's Home where I serve as chaplain. Pulling into the parking area, I noticed a young resident crying in front of the administration building. Inviting her into my office, I asked what was wrong.

Her answer? She loved living at Bethany. Amidst her tears, she went on to explain how wonderful it was to walk across campus and go to school without worry about being beaten or shot. Yet she feared for the safety of her brothers, sisters and cousins who still lived in "the projects." Two weeks later her cousin was shot and killed in a drive-by shooting.

Yet physical danger is no longer limited to public housing and inner cities. Violence has become a national scandal that has spread to rural villages, shopping malls and commuter trains.

When you look out your church door, are there people in danger? Are there those who suffer from child, spouse, or sexual abuse? Has violence become so endemic, that no one in your community is safe?

Your congregation might start or support a shelter for abused women and children or a training center for inner city youth. You might lobby for a ban on assault weapons, more police on the streets or tougher treatment for violent criminals. Sadly, there are limitless possibilities here for church involvement and conservatives should not be the only ones concerned for victims of violent crime.

Love And Belonging

Everyone needs to feel loved by family and friends, to feel they belong. Although the church has no monopoly here, in a society where so many feel isolated and alone, we have a critical role to play. Like Alcoholics Anonymous, churches can be "families of affiliation." Let me explain what I mean.

Recall in Matthew's gospel when Jesus is told his mother and brothers are looking for him.

> *But to the one who had told him this, Jesus replied, "Who is my mother, and who are my brothers?" And pointing to his disciples, he said, "Here are my mother*

and my brothers! For whoever does the will of my Father in heaven is my brother and sister and mother" (Matthew 12:48-50 NRSV).

Today, addiction specialists talk about "family of origin" and "family of affiliation." Simply, family of origin means the biological family into which we happen to be born. It may be healthy and loving or plagued by alcoholism and abuse. Whatever our biological family may be like, here we get no choice. Yet, as Jesus implies in Matthew's gospel, there are also families of affiliation, people we choose to make our family.

Looking out from your church, what do you see? Are there single parent families, neglected kids, aimless teens, searching young adults, lonely seniors? What vital ministries of community and connection, of family and friendship, could your church provide?

Are there possibilities for after school care for "latch key kids" at your church? Could you develop a new worship service targeted to meet the needs of searching young adults between 18 and 29 years of age? Informal services with interactive sermons and music backed by guitar, drums and synthesizers? Are there ways you can use the principles of the 8 Points/12 Steps to build friendship groups within your church? I suspect there are.

Self Worth

Each of us needs to believe we have value and worth. Clearly, this need can and must be addressed by the church.

However, we must draw a distinction between self esteem and self worth. Self esteem means the feeling of accomplishment that comes with success. The success may be a small one, like a child learning to tie his shoes. It may be a big one, like graduating from college. In any case, self esteem comes from achievement and feeling capable. No one can give self esteem; it must be won with effort and hard work.

Self worth is a different matter. Self worth is sheer grace. The confidence we are valuable before we get a chance to do, or fail to do, anything. Valued just for ourselves.

As we have seen, modern mass society values people who are useful, especially those who produce and consume. In sharp contrast, Liberal Christianity believes in human dignity, that every person is of value. Each is made a little lower than angels and in the image of God.

What do you see from your church door? Are there people in your community who need a word of encouragement and self worth? Could 8 Points/12 Step groups enable people to see forgiveness and love in other's eyes? Robert Schuller and his Crystal Cathedral rose to national prominence with this message. He argues there is great need for it and, obviously, he's right.

Self Actualization

For Maslow, the top rung of human need is self actualization. Here, we arrive at the spiritual issues of fulfillment, esthetics and world view. We reflect on questions of self and world, meaning and purpose, God and spirit.

How can the church address these higher needs? Today, modern advertising tells us to indulge and pamper ourselves. To find self fulfillment in consumption, pleasure and instant gratification. That is one kind of fulfillment, but as many are discovering, chasing after these gods eventually leaves us empty and disillusioned. To paraphrase the old Zen saying, "More things mean less."

Christianity understands our genuine need is for self fulfillment beyond selfishness. As Abelard suggested, contemplating Christ's suffering death can open the door to a spiritual awakening. We turn from too much concern with the world and its pleasures and toward devotion to the spiritual realm. Fulfillment comes from the spiritual goods of compassion, excellence, sacrifice, service, tolerance, mercy and simple delight in being alive. From a life well lived in accordance with the inner light God gives.

Second, Mainline churches can offer an understanding of the universe and our place in it. With so many competing world views, from fundamentalism, to consumerism, to New Age, we must make our basic message clear. The following is one statement of Liberal Christianity's ABC's:

> *1. A loving God has made all that is and wants every person to experience the joy of existence.*
>
> *2. Without God, the value, direction and goal of our lives is missing.*
>
> *3. Christ's death on the cross shows us how much God has loved us from the beginning.*
>
> *4. Turning our lives over to God's care in trust and obedience, we receive forgiveness, self worth and open the door to spiritual awakening.*
>
> *5. As part of God's community, we find friendship and fulfillment as we work together to spread God's love and remake the world in Christ's image.*

As you look in and around your church are people seeking these higher needs of fulfillment and meaning? Could your church offer educational opportunities to address Liberal Christianity's vision? Could you support taking liberal Christian ideals to Russia, Eastern Europe and the Third World? Could bulletin inserts at Sunday worship state liberal basics about God, Bible, individual conscience, human dignity and all the rest? Could our beliefs become as clear and well understood in our congregations as those in fundamentalist churches?

TOUGH DECISIONS

Liberal Christianity has a powerful vision and there is no shortage of need. But will congregations make the hard choices in order to respond? By temperament, many church people enjoy long established, time honored traditions. When asked, "How will we do it?" we answer, "Well, how did we do it last year?"

Yet, clearly, what we are doing now is not working and hasn't for years. If the Mainline church is to be renewed, or even to survive, new traditions must be established. However, psychologists tell us that no one changes very much and not at all without pain and hard work. You and I know this is especially true in the church.

What Went Wrong?

Let's begin with perhaps the most difficult and painful question the Mainline church must face. Why are Americans, and even our own church members, staying away in droves? Why are numbers and giving in a steady fall?

Consider, for example, a once prestigious congregation near my home. We'll call it Saint Bartholomew's. In 1952, its membership lists totaled 2,500. By 1962, that number had dipped to 1,800. By 1992, average Sunday morning attendance had plunged to 125. At the current rate of decline, this congregation will be gone within 20 years. Sadly, its story is repeated by hundreds of liberal, Mainline churches across America.

Why is this so? Is it simply because of populations shifts? Is it because Americans only want pleasure and entertainment? Don't we believe in God anymore? Has Christianity simply lost its appeal? Is our problem that only uneducated folk believe in Christianity and conservatives scoop them up with simplistic theology and slick marketing?

For a moment, let's suppose there is another answer. Perhaps we can learn a lesson from America's auto makers. Why did American car sales plunge in the 1980's? Was it because Americans no longer wanted cars? Had our love affair with the open road ended? Did cars suddenly seem silly, expensive and impractical? Did we learn to prefer public transportation, bicycles and walking instead?

No. While Big 3 sales were falling, Japanese cars made huge inroads into the American market. We still wanted cars; we just didn't want American ones. We wanted cars that were reliable, efficient, and attractive and Detroit wasn't building them.

How does this lesson apply to the church? I suggest the Big 3's problems are a metaphor of our own. Religion isn't dead, nor is Christianity. Surveys show that most Americans think Christianity might be relevant and important to their lives. Yet they also believe the churches in their neighborhood are irrelevant.

Like all humans, Americans still want and need love, belonging, self worth and fulfillment. However, like the Big 3, Mainline churches thought Americans would keep rushing through our doors no matter what we did. Like them, we were wrong.

For the past 20 years, Mainline leaders seemed to believe that if society found our ritual out of touch and our message irrelevant, it was their ignorance or sinfulness. If they found little programming that met their needs, they obviously wanted the wrong things. If our mission seemed weak, misdirected, or non-existent, they just did not understand our grand agenda.

Yet before we jump to these conclusions, it might be fruitful to take another look. What if people really do stay away because our message isn't relevant, clear or compelling? What if our program really doesn't meet important needs? Could it be our mission has lost its power and focus? What if the problem lies with us? Is it possible many Americans really do think liberal churches believe in nothing and stand for less?

The Big 3 automakers finally woke up. Will we? As harsh as it may sound, in the years ahead many local churches must decide. Either make the hard choices to build new traditions and meet real needs or die. And, like the two thieves crucified with Christ, such a death will be well deserved.

"Members Only" Or Advance Guard?

Here is a second painful question we must face. What is the church's role? During the Dark Ages the church became a fortress protecting the faithful from a hostile world. During the Medieval age, we saw it transformed into a mystical meeting place of heaven and earth. Yet if we are to impact modern society, our new Saint-Denis must be this and more. As Moltmann argues, we must become headquarters of the kingdom's advance guard. Again, we turn for instruction to Jesus' words.

> *He said to them, 'But who do you say that I am?' Simon Peter answered, 'You are the Messiah, the son of the living God.' And Jesus answered him, 'Blessed are you, Simon son of Jonah! For flesh and blood has not revealed this to you, but my Father in heaven. And I tell you, you are Peter, and on this rock I will build my church, and the gates of Hades will not prevail against it' (Matthew 16:15-18 NRSV).*

Although through the centuries Catholics and Protestants have vigorously debated Peter's role in this passage, we often missed Jesus' powerful metaphors for the church. First, we have the image of rock: stable, solid, fortress-like. In the next breath, however, the metaphor changes. We move from passive strength to violent assault. Yet, it is not the church that is under attack. Instead, the church is now pictured as a battering ram. Not an unmovable object but an invincible weapon against which even the gates of hell cannot stand.

Today, most Mainline congregations organize to serve their own members. There is little interest with those outside the church and no intentional effort to engage and attract them. Often, the attitude is "We're here and, if new people want to come, they can, if they fit in and don't make waves."

Churches whose sign board reads "Visitors Welcome" come to mind. Often, that is the only effort to recruit or welcome new members. If you know where the sanctuary and the rest rooms are, fine. If not, you are on your own. From the moment of entering, it's obvious this organization is for members only.

Yet in recent years, super churches like Saddleback Valley and Willow Creek Community Church became nationally famous for growth. These churches take exactly the opposite approach. They exist to reach new people. From worship and music to small groups, everything is designed to attract new members. Not surprisingly, they grow.

Although many liberal churches feel caught in a struggle for survival, those who try to save their lives, lose them. Those who try to hang on, lose out in the end. We must revive old traditions and create new ones that aggressively assault our age's spiritual, emotional and social problems. We must meet member's needs and intentionally engage and serve those outside the church. Live or die, that is our purpose for being.

A Question Of Identity

Finally, a last painful question. Some 30 years ago, American church historian Winthrop Hudson began predicting Mainline church decline because, he argued, denominations were losing their identity.

Of course, Hudson was right. Few people today join a congregation because it honors Luther's ideas, follows John Wesley's method or is a European ethnic church. In studies to determine why people join a particular local church, denominational loyalty hardly makes the list. Those days are gone.

For example, where I live in Pennsylvania, most United Church of Christ congregations grew from the German Reformed tradition. Three hundred years ago, Germans flocked to William Penn's holy experiment to find peace and religious tolerance.

These newcomers to Pennsylvania called themselves "Deutsch," in other words, Germans. The English speaking residents misunderstood this odd new language and thought these strangers were "Dutch." The name stuck. For generations, the Pennsylvania Dutch maintained their traditions and language separate from their English, Scotch, Irish, Welsh and Hungarian neighbors.

Today, the community's elders can still be heard speaking "Dutch" in southeastern Pennsylvania's country stores and post offices. Their "baby boomer" children, however, cannot speak "Dutch," although most can understand it. Their MTV generation grandchildren can do neither. These teenagers dress, act and speak just like those in California, Massachusetts or Colorado. American mass culture has absorbed them.

Admittedly, many church people long for our church's glory days, when Eisenhower was in the White House and all was right with the world. When we think of crowded pews and Sunday Schools we look to 1955, not 2010.

Yet no German Reformed nor any other ethnic European congregation can hope to survive planning to draw its members from a group that no longer exists. Likewise, no future exists for Presbyterian, Baptist or Episcopal churches hoping to advance ideas that were the burning issues in 1550 but are irrelevant today. If Mainline congregations are to be renewed, our basic identity must now come from a liberal Christian tradition that crosses ethnic and racial lines.

SUMMARY

Admittedly, ours is an enormous burden. Our goal is not to create a museum to past glories, but a living center for spiritual growth and world transformation. To continue rebuilding the Christian vision from Saint-Denis' rubble. To carve a human oasis from the modern world's spiritual wasteland. To rescue Western spiritual values from a bankrupt materialism. To safeguard humanity's future — and the future of life itself.

As awesome as these tasks may be, we cannot escape our destiny. To a generation facing the burden of civil war, Abraham Lincoln said, "We will be remembered in spite of ourselves. The fiery trial through which we pass will light us down in honor or dishonor to the latest generation. We ... hold the power and bear the responsibility."

Yet fortunately, our power comes from more than conscious will. As Gamaliel told the council in Jerusalem, "... if this plan or this undertaking is of human origin, it will fail; but if it is of God, you will not be able to overthrow them — in that case you may even be found fighting against God!" (Acts 5:38b-39 NRSV).

Epilogue

TOWERS IN THE LIGHT

A Final Word

Seen from a distance, the great cathedral at Chartres is an awe-inspiring sight. Silhouetted against a mellow golden twilight, its massive form dominates the town, its twin towers soaring into the sky. In Emile Mâle's words, it looks "... like a mighty ship about to set to sail on a long voyage."

Yet for all Chartres' magnificent beauty, it began with no more than a dream of what might be. Before the first windows were fashioned, the first statues carved, the Gothic vision had captured the imagination of Western Europe.

Great movements begin when, at the same moment in history, countless people are grasped by the same vision. The Reformation, the Industrial Revolution, the Space Age were all powered by an inspiring dream. Suddenly, many people in widely different places were stirred to action by an idea whose time had come.

Liberal Christianity has an inspiring vision. Now, like those who built the great cathedrals, we must make it reality.

As I began writing during the summer of 1992, I had only a vague idea of how this book might turn out, or who you, the reader, might be. But now, it seems a friend watches over my shoulder as these final words appear on the monitor screen. Many faces crowd my mind, those who have helped to shape and encourage my work. Yet none have helped as much as you.

We have traveled together from my study in Pennsylvania across the millennia and the universe itself. We pondered the time before the Big Bang. We sat for instruction at Jesus' feet. We learned from Abelard, Newton and Jung. Although perhaps we have never met and never will, I consider you a trusted friend.

Through our travels we have used Saint-Denis and the great cathedrals as a metaphor for Christianity's past, present and future. We do so again, one final time.

Of all the Medieval age's great rose windows, none surpass Chartres with its glorious colors and intricate images. Its circular form symbolizes the unity of God and humanity, heaven and earth, body and spirit. Within the circle, all opposites are reconciled. Its many colored glass pieces combine to form a pleasing, meaningful whole.

Chartres' rose window is symbolic of Liberal Christianity and our journey together. What is Liberal Christianity? It is the Divine Spirit working through the ages to build and tear down, to plant and pluck up, carrying out a plan hidden in the mind of God. It is Moses leading the Israelites from slavery, carrying the Ten Commandments down Mt. Sinai, dying before he reaches the Promised Land. It is the prophets' cry that justice roll like a river and righteousness like an everflowing stream.

It is Christ walking Palestine's dusty roads, teaching, blessing, healing, moving toward the cross. It is Easter morn and a stone rolled away. Saint Paul writing his letter to the church at Corinth long into the night. It is love and truth's victory over the Roman Empire's power, persecution and death.

It is Martin Luther, Johann Semler, Jane Addams, Walter Rauschenbusch, Martin Luther King, Jr., Caesar Chavez and Rosemary Ruether. It is the music of Bach, Mahalia Jackson and John Newton's hymn, "Amazing Grace." The art of Michelangelo, Raphael and millions of men and women who gave their devotion to churches across the world.

Everything and everyone can be used and useful in building the kingdom; in the divine economy, nothing is lost. All things work together for good for those who love God. Like Chartres' rose window, God's will and wisdom binds together all people, places and events in a meaningful whole.

While the metaphor of rose window whispers of receptivity, relatedness, and eternity, the Medieval cathedral's twin spires announce the importance of critical thinking and intentional action. Just as Christianity's past disappears in the mist of universal beginnings, the future continues to unfold toward its unforeseen goal. Together, we raise new cathedrals built from passionate commitment, clear thought and intentional action.

Perhaps you and I will not live to see our new Saint-Denis complete, yet we can make our contribution. We live in confidence that, someday, a new rose window will flood the world with magnificent colors. That, someday, towers will again stand gleaming in the light.

Ah. How glorious it will be.

STUDY GUIDE

Conversations

Despite the questions we have raised, one thing is certain. The time has come to open conversation within Mainline congregations about what we believe and should do. Hopefully, this study guide will foster useful discussion among church members and clergy.

Grouped by chapter and theme, some questions are more open-ended than others. It is not intended that every question be discussed, but that one or more might provoke useful conversation about the issues confronting the Mainline Church.

Feel free to make photocopies of these questions for distribution.

Chapter 1: A Pivotal Time

1. Do you think Liberal Christianity's ideals like freedom, responsibility, individual conscience, moral behavior, tolerance and democratic government, should play an important role in shaping the future?
2. Since communism's fall, what is your biggest fear for the world's future? Nuclear war? Terrorism? Crime? Ecological catastrophe? Something else?
3. How has instant global communications changed our view of Third World countries? How has it changed their view of North Americans?
4. As things stand now, who's vision will shape the future? That of fundamentalism? Scientific technology? Wall Street? Madison Avenue? Liberal Christianity?
5. Does it really matter if Mainline churches are clear about our beliefs?
6. In what ways does your church help its membership develop emotionally, intellectually and spiritually?
7. What is your church's mission?

Chapter 2: Abbot Suger To Hiroshima

1. Is science the most reliable guide to practical truth?
2. Are modern people more interested in this world than in heaven? Whatever your answer, why do you think this is so?
3. In what ways do you see the world and your life differently than your ancestors who lived in 1100 A.D.?
4. Some in the "Religious Right" want only conservative Christians and Jews in high government office. Do you?
5. The modern world has given people in the industrial countries many things. Are we too materialistic? As a society? As individuals? As a church?

Chapter 3: The Challenge Of Modern Science

1. Is it possible to be a modern, scientific person and a person of faith?
2. Can science answer all life's important questions? If it can't do so now, will it be able to do so someday?
3. What do we mean by the term "faith"? Is it believing literally in the Bible's supernatural stories despite scientific facts? Is it the beliefs we hold? Is it trust and loyalty toward God?
4. If you had to choose between trust in God or the benefits of modern science, medicine and technology, which would you choose?
5. Should "creation science" be taught in public schools?
6. Darwin argued that life evolved. Is evolution an accident or God's design?
7. How do you think God acts in history? By violating the laws of physics or is it by what science would call "natural means"?

Chapter 4: The Mystery Of Evil

1. An estimated 167,000,000 people have been killed in war or by political extermination during the 20th century. Can

we still believe that "God's in his heaven and all's right with the world"?

2. Chapter 4 suggests "the ant in the Persian rug" as a Christian explanation for suffering. Do you find it emotionally satisfying and reasonable?
3. If God could end suffering with one supernatural act, why not do it and do it now?
4. Chapter 4 suggests an alternative to the traditional Christian explanation of suffering. Here, God is all loving but limited in power. Do you find this explanation emotionally satisfying and reasonable?
5. Whatever the reason, there is suffering. How can we live with this fact?
6. What is the Christian responsibility toward those who suffer?

Chapter 5: The Bible

1. Is there more than one way to interpret the Bible?
2. Is it possible to live with computers, global communications and jet travel during the week and believe the Bible's supernatural stories are literally true on Sunday morning?
3. Who gets to decide what a biblical passage means? You? Your pastor or priest? Your church? The bishop? The "experts"?
4. Many in the "Religious Right" believe the Bible must be taken literally. Why don't they demand rebellious children be stoned to death as Deuteronomy 21:18-21 teaches?
5. What do you believe about the cross and resurrection? Are they historic fact or symbolic story? Can others hold a different position and still be Christian?
6. How much emphasis is placed on the Bible in your church? Why do you think that is so?

Chapter 6: Liberal Belief

1. Chapter 6 assumes there is a central core of liberal beliefs

and offers a suggested list. What would you add or remove? Would you prefer to throw this list out and start over?

2. In American society, freedom often means the right to do anything that is not illegal. Can liberal churches revive the idea that freedom is the right to follow God's will?
3. Do the rights and responsibilities of individuals really matter?
4. What is human nature? Are we basically good? Evil? A mix?
5. What are the moral standards of the liberal church?
6. Is Mahatma Gandhi burning in hell?
7. Some in the "Religious Right" want the church in charge of government. Do you? If so, which church should be in charge?

Chapter 7: A Liberal Spirituality

1. Does today's world seem stable and secure or chaotic and out of control?
2. Does an Alcoholics Anonymous group meet in your church? Do you know anyone who attends AA?
3. What do you feel is the most powerful argument for God's reality?
4. Is unresolved guilt a problem for people today? Does your church's current practice for dealing with guilt, whatever it is, provide real help?
5. Do you have a daily or regular spiritual routine?
6. How do you come to know God's will for your life?
7. Do you believe that God has a task for you?

Chapter 8: Teach Us To Build

1. Can Mainline church decline be stopped and reversed?
2. In a battle between the "gates of hell" and your church, who do you think would win? Why?
3. Considering Maslow's hierarchy, what needs does your church meet now? What more could your congregation do in your community? The nation? The world?

4. Is your church open to change?
5. Do you believe members in your church would be willing to make changes if they thought the church's survival was at stake? If vital human needs would go unmet?
6. What does your congregation do to intentionally engage and recruit new members?
7. How does your church's membership view your church and its mission? How do those in your community who are not members see your church?

ACKNOWLEDGMENTS

Shaped over a lifetime, it is impossible to mention all those whose thoughts have helped mold this book. Yet, some have had so special an influence I want to include them here.

I will always be grateful to Maurice Armstrong and Al Creager at Ursinus College who helped me see the possibilities in the Liberal tradition. At the Divinity Schools in Rochester, my deepest thanks to Kenneth Cauthen, Charles Nielsen and James Ashbrook whose wisdom, knowledge and guidance kept me on track. I hope that in some small way, I have made their penetrating insights, intense commitments and distinctive styles my own.

I am especially indebted to Ken Cauthen for his wise counsel while I was writing this book. Ken's suggestion that evil and suffering be more fully addressed led to Chapter 4. His views, first explained to me 20 years ago, frame the chapter. In addition, his willingness to write a foreword is appreciated more than I can say.

My thanks to Peter Goguts and George Fitz for years of conversation about the Liberal church's struggle and their suggestion that I seek publication for this book. Also, my thanks to Larry Lightfoot, Bethany's staff psychologist, who gave his scientific perspective on Chapter 3 and Rick Luciotti whose knowledge of Reality Therapy proved helpful with Chapter 4.

I am grateful for the distinctive talents of Russ Mitman, Merlin Getz, Barbara Kershner Daniel, Herman Ahrens, Mark Leidich, Ron Rhode and Homer Royer. Each helped in a unique way. My special thanks to Linda Gruber and Debbie Davis. Linda's keen insights helped me keep both the manuscript and my sanity in perspective. Debbie's own deeply felt inner quest helped me see the need for a straightforward statement of liberal beliefs.

I cannot possibly say enough about Bethany Children's Home. Garnet Adams and Harold Henning, the former and current directors, have given me a priceless opportunity to work with the boys, girls and staff who continually challenge, prod and provoke new insights.

It was William Pilder who introduced me to the writings of Carl Jung. For me, Jung is the 20th century's greatest Protestant thinker and his views play a major role in this book. Although Jung's collected works fill a substantial bookshelf, one slender volume written toward the end of his life called *The Undiscovered Self* stands out as especially important for Liberal Christianity.

This eloquent statement in defense of individuals against mass society's power ranges widely, delving into religious experience, myth, Christianity, communism and depth psychology. Its thoughtful approach is suggestive of ways to fill critical gaps in the Liberal tradition. Unfortunately, Jung never wrote "theology" and is rarely quoted outside the fields of pastoral care and counseling, but the Mainline church still has much to learn from him.

I cannot conclude without a word of thanks to the people of Churchville, United Methodist Church, Churchville, New York; Trinity and Saint Peter's UCC in Williams Valley, Pennsylvania; The Associated Church in Lisle, New York; and Trinity UCC, Rehrersburg, Pennsylvania. All tolerated my inept attempts to serve their churches. For their kindness and forbearance I will always be grateful.

INDEX